Reflective Teaching of Science 11–18

Also available from Continuum:

Readings for Reflective Teaching: Andrew Pollard

Reflective Teaching: Andrew Pollard

Reflective Teaching of History 11–18: Robert Phillips

Reflective Teaching of Science 3–11: Christina Farmery

Teaching Science with ICT: Len Newton and Laurence Rogers

Reflective Teaching of Science 11–18

Continuum Studies in Reflective Practice and Theory

John Parkinson

continuum
LONDON • NEW YORK

CONTINUUM
The Tower Building, 11 York Road, London SE1 7NX
370 Lexington Avenue, New York, NY 10017-6503

www.continuumbooks.com

First published 2002

British Library Cataloging-in-Publication Data
A catalogue record for this book is available from the British Library.
    ISBN 0-8264-5266-3 (hardback)
    ISBN 0-8264-5265-5 (paperback)

Typeset by SetSystems Ltd, Saffron Walden, Essex
Printed and bound in Great Britain by
MPG Books Ltd, Bodmin

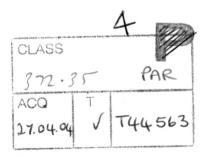

CONTENTS

ACKNOWLEDGEMENTS

I wish to express my gratitude to my colleagues in the Education Department of the University of Wales Swansea and to the science teachers involved in our initial teacher education partnership scheme. I am grateful to the science department at Porthcawl Comprehensive School for allowing me to include a photograph of part of their excellent wall display. I am indebted to the PGCE students with whom I have had the privilege to work with over the last twenty years. They have shown me that appropriate use of the teaching strategies described in this book enables effective learning to take place.

I have used examples of pupils' work and would like to thank Bethan Evans (Bishopston Comprehensive School) and Rachel and Beth Evans (Porthcawl Comprehensive School) for their help and contributions.

Finally I wish to thank the staff at Continuum for their help and support, particularly Anthony Haynes, Jo Yates and Christina Parkinson.

This book is dedicated to my family.

John Parkinson

CHAPTER 1

Learning to become an effective science teacher

INTRODUCTION

Learning about how to teach is a strange process. There are times when you think you have finally mastered it; everything is going well and you are riding on a high, then for no obvious reason the world crashes around you, nothing goes right and you fall into the depths of depression. In the early stages of teaching it is important to build up your own confidence about being in a classroom and interacting with a large number of individuals. This is an unusual situation for most new teachers, as previously they have only spoken to very small groups of people. As a teacher you have to communicate to a large number of people and learn how to relate to them in a professional manner. This chapter looks at the framework on which you can build your expertise in order to become a more effective science teacher.

By the end of this chapter you should:

- know about the qualities a good teacher requires;
- understand what contribution science can make to the education of young people;
- appreciate what pupils like and dislike about science;
- be able to reflect on the quality and effectiveness of your own teaching;
- understand the professional requirements of teachers.

1 WHAT MAKES A GOOD SCIENCE TEACHER?

To answer this question you might think back to someone who inspired you to study science. Many of you starting in the teaching profession will have been motivated by someone who taught you at school and you may have a desire to incorporate some of the characteristics of that teacher into your own teaching style. To be a good science teacher you need to appreciate the learning needs of all your pupils and the value in their lives of the science you are teaching them, both in school and as adults. Some of your pupils will go on to use science as part of their jobs but the majority will not. You will need to cater for all pupils' needs. The following list (adapted from Harris *et al.*, 1996), gives the main characteristics of a good science teacher. A useful way of using the list is to periodically review your progress by considering the extent to which your teaching matches each of the points.

Good science teachers:

- *are enthusiastic about science* – your enthusiasm is likely to rub off on your pupils. Good teachers show an interest in the science that is being taught. They provide positive role models of scientific curiosity, competence and creativity. They are confident about learning alongside the pupils they teach;

- *are knowledgeable about the science they teach* – good teachers make sure that they thoroughly understand the scientific concepts they are going to teach. They are able to deal with pupils' questions and provide background information, anecdotes and further examples, etc. to promote pupils' interest;

- *are clear about their teaching goals* – teachers need to know exactly what they want the pupils to learn by the end of the lesson. This helps to produce a clear plan of carefully timed activities;

- *are able to communicate to their pupils what is expected of them* – good teachers convey the goals of the lesson to the pupils;

- *address higher, as well as lower, order cognitive objectives* – good teachers encourage imaginative and personally original thinking. They ensure that pupils are capable of answering different types of questions from simple recall of knowledge to questions involving the use of analytical skills;

- *teach pupils metacognitive strategies and give them opportunities to master them* – pupils need to have an understanding of their own learning if they are to make good progress;

- *are able to deploy a wide variety of teaching strategies* – good teachers make expert use of the teaching materials available. They make sure that pupils are busy carrying out tasks and learning during each lesson;

- *are knowledgeable about their pupils and their learning needs* – good teachers make sure that their teaching strategies match the goals for the lesson and are suitable for the age and ability range of the pupils. They anticipate pupils' misconceptions and use strategies to help them learn the correct science. They have high expectations of their pupils and make these explicit to the individuals concerned;

- *monitor pupils' understanding through regular, appropriate feedback* – good teachers give frequent written and oral feedback to pupils on their classroom contributions and homework. They make sure that work is complete and correct and give encouragement for pupils to improve their performance. They recognize that pupils' results depend on their ability to teach as well as the pupils' ability to learn;

- *use pupils' own ideas* – good teachers demonstrate openness, sensitivity and a willingness to take young people's ideas and question them seriously;

- *are thoughtful and reflective about their practice* – good teachers recognize the need for personal and professional development.

Earlier I raised the point of teaching science to all pupils and some of you may have wondered why we can't just teach it to those that are interested and leave the others to follow courses that interest them. Wellington (2000) provides us with some very sound reasons for studying science that he divides roughly into three categories: the intrinsic worth of learning science; its extrinsic or utility value; and arguments concerned with citizenship.

1. *The intrinsic value of science education*
   Everyone wants to know something about themselves as a human being, something about how things work in their immediate environment and, quite often, something about the world and beyond. Science is about finding out new things and, as such, it is a particularly interesting and exciting subject. Science can also be seen as an important cultural pursuit and one could argue that everyone needs to know about this strand of culture in order to make them a rounded individual.

2. *The extrinsic or utility value*
   It is clearly of value to those who go on to follow careers that require a science background, but it will also provide all pupils with a range of useful skills. For example, pupils will learn how to approach problems scientifically. They should learn about different quantities and dimensions and have an understanding of scale and magnitude of units. One would also hope that science courses would help pupils to see the value of science and the need to go on learning about our universe.

3. *Science for citizenship*
   In order to contribute to debate on scientific issues, individuals need to have a basic scientific knowledge and know where to go to find further information. They also need to know something about the discipline itself, how scientists work, the nature of evidence and the interpretation of results. In other words they need to have an understanding about the nature of science.

Practical activity 1.1

It is worthwhile asking yourself, from time to time, why are you teaching science to a particular class and then to consider if the type of science you are teaching them is appropriate to their needs.

In addition to the ITT standards, you could use the list of characteristics of good teachers as a framework for monitoring your progress.

2 PUPILS' LIKES AND DISLIKES

Pupils tend to have fairly strong views about what they like or dislike in their lessons. You may initially think that they like lessons that are a 'skive' and don't like lessons where they have to work. On the whole this is untrue. They like to feel a sense of achievement, that they have accomplished something new rather than wasted their time. Creating the ideal classroom environment is difficult for a new teacher. While pupils like working in a controlled environment where the teacher is clearly in charge they do not like working under very rigid conditions where they are afraid to ask questions. They like an atmosphere that is relatively relaxed, where discipline is maintained and where they feel happy to approach the teacher for further help if they don't understand. Pupils like teachers with a sense of humour, someone who is prepared to share a joke with the class and who is prepared to laugh at him/herself. By and large they appreciate teachers who put a lot of effort into the preparation of teaching materials and they certainly value the fact that you have made the effort to make the work interesting. Pupils like to be known as a person and they set great store by you calling them by their name.

Osborne and Collins (2001) have carried out a large-scale investigation into pupils' views about science and these are summarized below.

2.1   Aspects of science that pupils liked

- Biology topics included:
  o human biology;
  o aspects conceived as being more modern, e.g. the effects of drugs.
- Chemistry topics included:
  o mixing chemicals and seeing the effects for themselves (particularly liked the element of danger);
  o situations where there was some choice and pupils had to make decisions.
- Physics topics included:
  o space;
  o forces in relation to cars and flight (boys);
  o light and electricity (girls).
- Practical work.
- Being challenged and stimulated to learn more.

2.2   Aspects of science that pupils disliked

- The apparent 'low tech' nature of some of the subject matter (e.g. the blast furnace).
- The sense that they have to rush through the curriculum (there isn't enough time, everything has to be done in a hurry).
- The remoteness of some aspects of science (particularly aspects of chemistry, e.g. the periodic table).
- Copying (seen as 'boring writing').
- Being told to accept things rather than have them explained.
- The emphasis on learning lots of facts.
- The repetition of work.
- A lack of time for discussion and putting forwards your own views.
- Lack of opportunity to be creative (work done within fairly tight limits, pupils not given the opportunity to express themselves).
- The fragmentation of the curriculum (poor links between the different components of a science course).

> ### Practical activity 1.2
>
> Review your teaching of one topic over a period of five to ten lessons and highlight the times that you have carried out things in the 'pupils dislike' list above.
>
> How could you have made your lessons more interesting for the pupils?
>
> To what extent were you helping them to become good future citizens?
>
> What messages did you give about the way in which scientists work?

3   PROFESSIONAL ATTITUDES AND RESPONSIBILITIES

As soon as you enter your school as a trainee teacher you take on a whole new set of responsibilities. While in school you need to conduct yourself in a manner that you would expect of a teacher. Like it or not, you become a role model for a large number of young people. If you take little pride in your appearance, why should they? If you arrive late for lessons, they may do the same. If you don't mark their homework on time, why should they bother to hand it in on time? Being a teacher requires a high level of professional conduct and commitment. Figure 1.1 gives a broad outline of the sorts of things you would be expected to do during school experience but it is advisable to check to see if your school has any additional rules. The General Teaching Councils have been set up to promote high standards of professional practice and conduct and have each produced a Professional Code for teachers. Once you become a qualified teacher you will be required to become a member of one of the Councils and will be obliged to comply with the Code.

It goes without saying that your teaching should be of a good standard and that, within reason, you should do everything you can to help pupils to learn. You also need to build that special teacher–pupil relationship with the young people in your care. This can be quite difficult for some young student teachers, who find themselves becoming over friendly with the pupils. You need to create some distance between yourself and those who you teach. If you find that the pupils go to the same clubs or pubs that you do, then I suggest you change and go somewhere else. You may be flattered by the attention given to you by some youngsters – resist the temptation!

During your time in school you are a member of two very important teams – the Science Department team and the Pastoral team – as well as having duties relating to the whole school. As a member of the Science Department you will need to make yourself familiar with all its routines and procedures. You will be expected to contribute, by doing things and involving yourself with its activities. This will help you to get a wider view of what is required of a science teacher and help you to build up relationships with your colleagues. In a very small minority of cases, student teachers don't hit it off with members of the department. In such cases you need to keep trying, helping out wherever and whenever you can and make sure you are not found in the prep room reading the daily

Punctuality	You should arrive at school in plenty of time before the start of the school day and, whenever possible, arrive early for lessons.
Time on site	Unless you are given permission to leave, you should be on the school site all of the school day.
Attendance	If, for any reason, you cannot attend school you should let the school know in advance and provide work for those classes you would have taken.
Appearance	You should be clean and tidily dressed (pupils are very quick to pick up on body odour and what you wear).
Relationships with pupils	As a teacher you are a leader and as such there must always be some distance between yourself and your pupils. Do not ask pupils personal questions and refuse to answer their personal questions. An exception to this would be when a pupil comes to you with a personal problem.
Relationships with staff	Show respect for your teaching colleagues and it is likely that they will respect you. Appreciate that full-time teaching staff are very busy and they may not be able to see you just when you want. Be cooperative. Share your views and experiences with colleagues.
Assessment and marking	Apply the system used by other science teachers. Do not allow pupils to cheat. Keep accurate records and pass them on to the appropriate teacher.
Relationship with parents/guardians	You should appreciate the mechanisms in place for communicating with parents and comply with them. You should attend parents' evenings.

Figure 1.1 *General guidelines for professional conduct of student teachers*

paper when everyone else is rushing around teaching. Being a member of the Pastoral team gives you the opportunity to meet with teachers from other disciplines and talk to them about their perspectives on teaching. You will also be able to contribute to a different aspect of pupils' learning and develop an understanding of how the pastoral programme intermeshes with the academic curriculum.

4   SUBJECT KNOWLEDGE

Having a good grasp of the subject is a pre-requisite for good teaching, but how can you judge that your knowledge is good enough? Those of you who have done well in school examinations and obtained a good degree may feel fairly confident that you know what you are talking about. However, there is quite a lot of evidence to show that even this group of people demonstrate significant insecurity in their understanding of certain branches of science. When you are preparing to teach a topic it is advisable to spend some time reading, not just at the level you are going to teach but also at higher levels. When doing this you need to question yourself, asking why things happen and how you would explain particular scenarios. You should see the development of your subject knowledge as an on-going process. You need to remind yourself of science concepts and you will need to keep up to date with developments in your subject specialism. Being a learner, alongside the pupils, can help to bring a freshness to lessons and help to generate excitement and enthusiasm.

Practical ativity 1.3

Monitor your subject knowledge by carrying out some, or all, of the following:

- Photocopy the pages for KS3 & KS4 from the National Curriculum and carry out a self-audit of subject knowledge by marking each section using a scale of understanding such as 1 = confident, 2 = unsure, 3 = no knowledge.
- Work through a GCSE science paper (making sure you cover all areas of the National Curriculum) and an A-level paper in your science specialism. Compare your answers with the ones provided by the board.
- Prepare a concept map (see p. 77) for each topic that you teach. By looking at the links between ideas and the number of ideas you have identified for the topic you will be able to get a sense of your depth of understanding.
- Find out about the common misconceptions held by pupils for the topic (see Driver *et al.*, 1994a, 1994b) and compare these with your own understanding.

5 KNOWLEDGE ABOUT TEACHING

You will have a number of preconceived ideas about teaching when you enter your teacher education course and probably one of the first things that you will have to appreciate is that not everyone learns in the same way that you do. Another aspect of teaching that student teachers don't always understand is that it takes a long time to become an effective practitioner and that the learning process is far from linear. You may find that you are making great strides in your teaching and then, for all sorts of reasons, things begin to go horribly wrong. There will be a 'honeymoon' period where the pupils will be a little unsure of you and will be on their best behaviour, followed by a time when they test you out to see how far they can go. You may also go through a period where you become very confident with your own performance and you decide that you don't need to prepare in so much detail. As a result the quality and sharpness of the lessons may decline and pupils' motivation and behaviour take a downturn.

You can learn about teaching by:

- thinking about your own experiences as a learner;
- observing experienced teachers at work (see Parkinson, 1994, pp. 53–6, for guidance on lesson observation);
- reading about approaches to teaching and how pupils learn;
- attending lectures/seminars/pre-service and in-service courses;
- discussing your lessons with mentors and tutors;
- reflecting on your own teaching performance.

Most of this seems obvious, and you will start doing it as soon as you begin your teacher education course, but the idea of reflecting on your performance as a teacher deserves more explanation. A great deal has been written about reflection in teaching (e.g. Pollard and Triggs, 1997; Schön, 1991) concerned with what it is and how to do it. A reflective teacher is someone who thinks about what goes on in the classroom, makes an appraisal of the situation and then uses the information to improve. On one level this may simply be taking into account something that happened during the lesson and remembering to do it differently next time. On a deeper level it involves a rigorous analysis of what has happened during the lesson by asking the question 'why?' Lessons are very complicated situations with lots of things going on at once and, initially, it will be difficult for you to identify the key events. As you become more relaxed in the classroom, and as you gain experience of analysing situations through the feedback you are given by other teachers, your ability to monitor what is going on will rapidly improve. One way of training yourself to gather evidence about your teaching is to restrict the focus of your reflection to one or two areas, e.g. classroom control, the organization of practical work, the use of praise. Another problem that faces student teachers is that of making judgements on the quality of their work. Depending on your outlook on life, you may think that everything has gone brilliantly when in fact it hasn't, or you may think it was a terrible lesson when really it wasn't bad at all. So how do you make judgements when you have no real yardstick to help you? Is it fair to compare your performance with someone who has been in the profession for years? Although there is no absolute measuring instrument, your attention should be focused on the pupils, the experiences they have and the learning they achieve. At first it is likely that certain incidents will dominate your thinking. For example, a breach of discipline that takes you by surprise can lead to a clouding of your judgement about the whole lesson. You are likely to go through a number of stages of reflection, as illustrated in Figure 1.2. As your experiences grow you will become able to analyse situations objectively and your ability to learn from your experiences will improve. One way of helping you to gain the necessary skills is to compare your impression of a lesson with those of an experienced teacher. In your discussion you would probably cover the following:

- What have you assumed about the pupils in terms of:
  - o prior knowledge

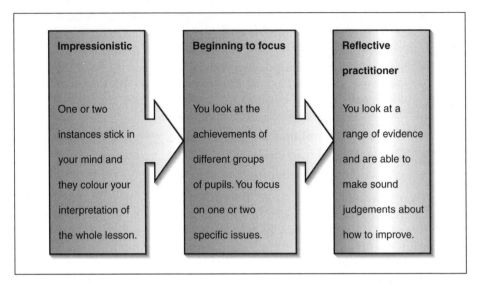

Figure 1.2 *Stages in the reflective process*

    o ability to understand
    o ability to carry out tasks
    o standard of written work
    o temperament
    o concentration span/attentiveness
    o doing homework?

● What aspects of the lesson did you think went well and what went less well? As a keen new teacher you will be disappointed when things go wrong, and so you need to celebrate your successes and be able to identify where and why things went wrong. It is sometimes difficult to get at the 'why' part and you may have to tease this out by discussion with the person who observed the lesson. In the early part of your school experience the focus of the feedback is likely to be on your performance as a teacher but as time goes on the focus will change and become more concerned with the pupils' learning experiences.

● What aspects of the feedback are specific to that class/situation/topic and what is generalizable? You need to know this so that you avoid getting into situations where you put into practice something you have been told in a previous lesson, only to be told again that you are doing things incorrectly.

As you progress you will need to start thinking about how you can determine the quality of a lesson. It is not uncommon for student teachers to think they have had a good lesson if all the pupils have been well behaved and have listened quietly to what they have said. While good class control is an essential part of teaching, having a well-behaved class doesn't necessarily mean that the pupils have learnt anything. So you will have to look for additional pieces of evidence to judge the effectiveness of your teaching, such as:

- Are the pupils enjoying what they are going? Do they seem to be motivated and keen to get on with the work you have set? When you move around the class, during a group activity, are pupils talking about the work?

- How well do pupils respond to your oral questions? How keen are they to let you know that they have understood the work (bearing in mind that some older pupils may be reluctant to answer questions in front of their peers)? What sort of questions do pupils ask you?

- Do pupils carry out practical work sensibly with due attention to safety?

- What is the quality of their written work? Is it complete, neat and correct?

- How well do pupils perform in written tests?

Over a period of time you will improve your teaching skills, provided you listen carefully to the advice given to you and act upon it. Alongside that, and clearly inter-related with it, you will need to make progress in your ability to reflect on your teaching in order for you to continue to develop as a teacher once the support structure of the initial teacher education programme has been removed. Figure 1.3 summarizes the cyclical process of reflection, moving through the planning and teaching of a lesson to collecting and analysing evidence on its effectiveness that can be used to inform future teaching. In order to have a firm foundation for reflection you not only need classroom experience, you need to have a good understanding about teaching and learning science. This will come from your university work, the reading you do and the interactions you have with experienced teachers.

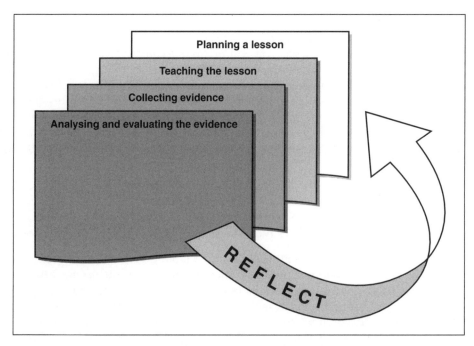

Figure 1.3 *The process of reflective teaching*

Practical activity 1.4

Early on in your teaching experience

Consider how you are going to reflect on one or two aspects of your teaching:

- your distribution of questions around the class;
- your use of a variety of questions;
- your responses to pupils' answers;
- the quality of pupils' responses.

Consider how you would collect evidence for these points.

Later on in your teaching experience

Get an overview of the quality of a lesson by completing a self-evaluation form and then look at one or two areas in more detail. A self-evaluation form might cover the following areas with space for you to give your level of satisfaction with your performance:

- subject knowledge
- planning and preparation
- availability of resources
- starting the lesson
- your communication skills
- use of blackboard /ohp/IT
- management of activities
- timing and pace
- monitoring of pupils' understanding
- monitoring of pupils' progress
- control and discipline
- ending of the lesson
- quality of the pupils' learning
- your enthusiasm and interaction
- the pupils' enthusiasm and interest

Towards the end of your teaching experience

Evaluate the quality of the pupils' learning through a study of their oral and written contributions to lessons. Are they able to recall information you gave them correctly? Are they able to go beyond that and use information in a variety of ways? Is there any indication that they have found out additional information for themselves? Have the pupils been able to monitor their own learning?

6 | DEVELOPING CRITICAL REFLECTION

The type of reflection described above requires you to deliberately undertake an inquiry to improve your teaching. The process, usually described as reflection on-action, is most useful when it is carried out critically. This is when you start scratching below the surface and begin to identify reasons for things happening. To do this you need to step back from the classroom and try to use what you have learnt from a variety of sources in order to analyse the situation. Frequently, this is one of the purposes of writing assignments in initial teacher education courses. One example of this type of reflective tool is the production of a portfolio. This should contain examples of your own and pupils' work together with a commentary. You should include examples of things that went well and things that didn't go so well. This sort of activity is useful at helping you to look for appropriate evidence and think about ways of interpreting it. You may also find it useful to take material from the portfolio when you go for a teaching post interview. Another example is the production of a reflective diary or journal where you log experiences and comment on them. This gives you the opportunity to follow things through over a period of time. You could choose to either have this as a strictly personal form of reflection or, if you wish, use it as the basis for a dialogue with your mentor or other students in a seminar.

The process of learning about teaching never ends, and you may find it useful to think about incorporating some sort of systematic research of what goes on in your classroom in order to be able to structure your development. This approach to teaching is encouraged by universities and the Teacher Training Agency (TTA, 1999) who are able to offer help and support.

CONCLUSION

Some students find it very easy to slip into the mode of being a teacher but it can be a major challenge for others. For the new graduate there can be the shock of moving from a fairly relaxed atmosphere as an undergraduate to a more regimented approach in school. For the person who has come from a senior position in industry or commerce there are problems of a change in status and appreciating that some of the methodology used in the world of business doesn't always easily translate into school life. Coming to terms with these changes and appreciating that change is an important aspect of education is in itself a useful piece of learning. Teachers are constantly having to deal with change, either imposed by the government or school or because they themselves see it as necessary. It is this variety that makes it one of the most interesting jobs available. Put alongside this, the fact that you are helping to prepare a considerable number of young people for adult life makes it an extremely rewarding job.

CHAPTER 2

Pupils' learning in science

INTRODUCTION

For most students starting an initial teacher education course, ideas about learning tend to be very naïve. Perhaps this is not altogether surprising as you are unlikely to have made a study of learning or have spent little time thinking about it except in terms of how you learn. The purpose of this chapter is to make you aware of the key research findings about pupils' learning, a knowledge of which is essential for effective teaching.

By the end of this chapter you should:

- understand that there are different types of learners;
- appreciate the contributions made by a number of educational psychologists to learning theories;
- use ideas about pupils' learning in the planning of lessons.

1   TEACHING AND LEARNING

It comes as a surprise to a lot of young teachers when a significant number of pupils in a class appear to have no recollection of what they have just been taught. It might be expected if there had been a reasonable time gap, but sometimes pupils are unable to answer questions even fifteen minutes after they have been taught. You may have felt that your delivery was good and your explanations superb. Why then did the pupils not learn? It is easy to get drawn into the trap of believing that the pupils will soak up all the wisdom coming from you, and be able to regurgitate it at a later date. Learning is something that pupils must do for themselves and what the teacher has to do is to set up situations that will promote learning. Figure 2.1 depicts the traditional view of the teacher as transmitter of knowledge with the pupil sitting attentively, waiting to receive new ideas about science. This may work for some pupils but for others this is little more than a nice time to sit, relax and think of other things.

A science teacher who taught in this way would consider that his/her lessons were good if:

- *the pupils listened quietly to what was being said* – this is only of value if the pupils understood and were able to make sense of what was being said. There may be pupils who look attentive but their minds may be focused on something quite different from the science you are teaching;
- *s/he 'got through' a lot of the subject matter in any one lesson* – this is of no

Figure 2.1 *Instruction viewed as the direct transmission of knowledge*

value unless the pupils have the opportunity to demonstrate that they understand the work. Sometimes teachers think that their pupils are 'soaking up' all that they are telling them when the truth is that the learning is fragile or non-existent;

- *the syllabus was finished quickly* – finishing the syllabus without ensuring proper understanding is of no merit. Pupils may become disaffected as they spend the time gained going through the same work in revision lessons;
- *the pupils are able to answer examination questions* – this might be possible if pupils have been subjected to drill and practice activities but it is unlikely that they will be able to answer questions requiring the use of higher order cognitive skills.

In order to make your teaching effective you need to know something about the ways pupils learn. It may not be as simple as making sure that everyone is paying attention by carefully monitoring the expressions on their faces, although that helps. It will involve using a range of techniques to make sure that you cover the learning needs of individuals in your class.

You also need to think about the depth of learning. In some situations you may only want your pupils to learn by rote. For example, they will have to remember the colour of light in the visible spectrum and the list of characteristics of living things and the easiest way of remembering these is to learn a mnemonic (e.g. ROYGBIV, MRS GREN). This level of learning enables the pupils to recall information but has little influence on deeper learning. For example, a pupil may be able to recall that respiration is one of the characteristics of living things but may not be able to describe what respiration is, due to a lack of understanding.

It was the educational psychologist David Ausubel that first made the distinction between rote learning and meaningful learning. When meaningful learning occurs there is a greater in-depth understanding of the concept and the pupil is able to link the new area of knowledge with existing knowledge. Ausubel (1968) also made the distinction between the passive learning situation, as shown in Figure 2.1, and learning by discovery. Attempts at planning teaching based on a discovery approach were tried out in the period 1960–70 but they largely failed. There were a number of reasons for this. Pupils sometimes became frustrated with the process and asked the teachers to give them the right answer, and sometimes they didn't discover what they were supposed to discover. Pupils sensed that the whole process was false and that they were going though a lengthy procedure for no apparent gain. Nowadays we tend to restrict the use of discovery learning to certain types of open investigations (see p. 125) where pupils are truly finding things out for themselves. In this type of work the learning of new scientific concepts may not be the prime objective. Pupils will be learning about scientific methodology as they examine ways of doing their experiments.

If meaningful learning is to take place, then the teacher needs to set up situations where the pupils have the opportunity to reflect on the new knowledge and use it. So rather than being passive recipients they need to become active learners. Much of this book is devoted to activities that promote active learning through pupils' writing, talking and practical activity. In these situations the teacher is not only a supplier of information but a person who guides and supports individuals as they try to make sense of scientific concepts.

2 | DIFFERENT TYPES OF LEARNERS

Just as you will have classes of pupils who are mixed in terms of their ability to learn you will also have pupils who like learning in different ways. You need to be aware of this in planning your work over a period of time. If your lessons contain the same sort of activity time after time then you may be motivating only a small fraction of the class. A variety of teaching approaches will ensure that you capture the imagination of a broader cross-section of the pupils. There are a number of different ways of looking at preferred learning styles but all have some common themes. Bishop and Denley (1997) provide us with some useful pen portraits of different learners based on the work of David Kolb. There are four typical groups of learners.

Dynamic learners:
- like to try things out and don't worry about getting it wrong;
- enjoy variety and look for excitement;
- are keen to take action and get others involved;
- don't want to plan and don't want to check work;
- manage their time badly.

Common sense learners:
- read instructions carefully and organize their time well;
- enjoy solving problems by integrating theory and practice;
- work well alone, are thorough and decisive;
- like doing things their way but are not very imaginative;
- want to get the job done but don't like being given answers.

Imaginative learners:
- like to see the whole picture and the relationship between ideas;

- enjoy brainstorming sessions and using their imagination;
- listen well and like group work;
- work in fits and starts and forget important detail;
- are easily distracted and indecisive.

Analytical learners:

- are well organized and can work alone;
- are analytical and logical and see the links between ideas;
- see clear goals and apply theories to problems;
- don't like group discussion;
- get bogged down in detail.

(Bishop and Denley, 1997, p. 19)

These characteristics give a broad picture of how each type of learner responds to learning situations. With these sorts of categorizations you mustn't get bogged down in detail – people don't need to match each one of the bullet points under one heading to be classified as that type of learner.

There are a host of other things in addition to the pupils' preferred learning style that are likely to affect the quality and extent of learning. These include:

- the nature of the teacher–pupil relationship;
- the ability of the teacher to create and maintain an atmosphere for learning;
- the physical classroom environment and personal space;
- interaction with other people, before, during and after the lesson.

All of these are discussed in other parts of the book.

Practical activity 2.1

Carry out a small-scale investigation into pupils' preferred learning styles either by selecting three or four pupils and observing them over a two to three week period or by devising a short questionnaire that you give to a class at a suitable time (say registration period, during a PSE period on learning, when you going to talk about study skills). Discuss the results with your mentor and consider the implications for your teaching.

3   DIFFERENT TYPES OF INTELLIGENCE

Closely related to pupils' learning style is the idea of intelligence. You could quite simply say that a person who is good at your subject is intelligent. But sometimes individuals excel at some things but not at others. You might say that David Beckham and Paul Gascoigne use the ball intelligently in their football but you might equally say they are not intelligent in other ways. 'IQ' tests have been used as a measure of intelligence for many years but many now think that this value gives a very narrow and not particularly useful measure. Howard Gardner's work provides us with a model of intelligence that goes well beyond the naïve IQ approach and provides us with a framework for planning teaching (Gardner, 1983). He identifies seven areas of intelligence:

- interpersonal
- intrapersonal
- kinaesthetic
- linguistic
- mathematical and logical
- musical
- visual and spatial.

We all have strengths and weaknesses in each of these areas and our profile of strengths may be one of the reasons why we preferred to study science at school rather some of the other subjects. Now you have to ask yourself the question: 'Is my role to foster the interests of pupils who, like me, are going to follow the science route (i.e. predominantly mathematical and logical learners) or am I trying to interest all pupils in science?' If you are interested in helping all pupils to gain an understanding of science (and I hope you are) then, as you can see, you need to try to cater for the range of different needs. Figure 2.2 lists the characteristics of the separate intelligences and matches them to the sort of learning activity that would most suit that type of pupil. It strengthens the argument for including a variety of activities in science lessons in order to benefit from the wide range of expertise amongst the pupils and to maintain an interest in science.

4 | AGES AND STAGES: THE WORK OF PIAGET

Jean Piaget spent his working life researching into the tasks that children can do at various ages (Flavell, 1963). He believed that children actively construct knowledge through their everyday experiences and through teaching. This knowledge is then assimilated into a child's cognitive structure. Sometimes the experiences may be at odds with the child's current understanding and he or she may change or accommodate the existing cognitive structure. These two processes of assimilation and accommodation are seen as essential in helping the child to understand the world and to develop intellectually. Piaget believed that this development took place in a number of stages, which he named:

- preoperational, labelled 1
- early concrete, labelled 2A
- mature (or late) concrete, labelled 2B
- early formal, labelled 3A
- mature (or late) formal, labelled 3B.

Concrete operations refer to the simple processes of science, such as classifying, manipulating single variables, and recognizing the simple cause and effect

	Characteristics	Linked learning activities
Interpersonal	Relate well to others Are at ease in groups Are prepared to take on the role of team leader	Group work (be on the look out for over-dominance of the group) Contribution to class discussion (be on the look out for hogging the conversation) Concept mapping through group discussion Peer teaching/cooperative learning Role play
Intrapersonal	Often enjoy working alone They are metacognitive learners (see p. 31)	Researching a topic by themselves Homework Thinking up questions for the teacher to answer Working alone on the computer Setting personal targets for improvement Preparing their own concept maps
Kinaesthetic	Are good at sport, good hand–eye coordination Are good at dance Can be restless if required to sit still for long periods	Role play Practical tasks Model building Science quizzes and games Identifying key words in a text
Linguistic	Enjoy communicating, sometimes through writing and talking and sometimes just through one method Are good at spelling Have a good vocabulary	Creative writing Role play DART exercises Researching a topic by themselves Contribution to class discussion
Mathematical and logical	Are good with numbers See patterns easily Organized in their approach to work Measure things accurately Adopt a problem-solving approach to tasks	Calculations Organizing work, e.g. preparing summary diagrams and lists, flow charts, creating links between related topics Producing graphs and charts Using computers
Musical	Enjoy listening to, and sometimes playing, music Have a good appreciation of rhythm and movement Appreciate that word and sound groupings can often lead to change in mood and feeling	Writing poems, raps, etc. Learn with background music Use music to relieve stress
Visual and spatial	Have artistic talent Are able to easily visualize things in three dimensions Can easily find their way around text	Model building Preparing visual displays Identifying key points in texts with appropriate markers Role play Drawing and interpreting diagrams

Figure 2.2 *Gardner's multiple intelligences: linking characteristics of the learner to appropriate learning activities* (adapted from The Learners' Cooperative, 1998)

relationships. Formal operations involve using science to develop and understand situations. Figure 2.3 gives you an indication of what you would expect a pupil to be able to do at each of the stages. More detailed information for most of the topics taught at key stages 3 and 4 can be found in Shayer and Adey (1981).

Pupils do not pass through these stages uniformly and, in fact, may not reach the higher levels at all. Research carried out in the late 1970s by Philip Adey and Michael Shayer, using Science Reasoning Tasks (SRTs), on a large sample of pupils in England and Wales gave some rather disturbing results:

- In the population as a whole, fewer than 30 per cent of 16 year-olds were showing the use of even early formal operations (3A). That means that the majority of the population was leaving school using only concrete operations.
- The range of levels of thinking within any one age group was far wider than had previously been realised ... In ordinary mixed-ability high schools, the most able 12 year-olds were operating at the level of average 18 year-olds or higher and the least able at the level of average 6 year-olds.

(Adey and Shayer, 1994, p. 31)

Figure 2.4 shows the distribution of Piagetian levels in boys from the age of 4 to 18 for those of average ability and the top and bottom 5 per cent. This clearly shows the spread of cognitive development at any one age.

Using the SRTs it is possible to determine the operational Piagetian level of a pupil. It is also possible to study a science topic and work out its cognitive demand (i.e. what level a pupil would need to be operating at to fully understand it). This is not too difficult an exercise and you are invited to have a go yourself in Practical Activity 2.2. Adey and Shayer (1994) have carried out this sort of analysis for the 1991 version of the science National Curriculum and have shown that the higher levels require pupils to operate at the formal level.

If you want to find out more about the life and work of Piaget try typing in his name into one of the web search engines. You may be surprised at the amount of information you can get on this one man.

Practical activity 2.2

Carry out an analysis of one of your lessons in terms of the cognitive demand required of the pupils. Look at what type of cognitive processes you want your pupils to use and use Figure 2.3 to give you the Piagetian level that is nearest match to the mental operations you have identified. If you have access to a 1991 version of the Science National Curriculum you might be able to compare your analysis with that given in Adey and Shayer (1994, p. 35).

5 LEARNING WITH THE HELP OF OTHERS

The emphasis of Piaget's work was the interaction of the child with events in his/her own environment. Another psychologist, Lev Vygotsky, provided us with

Stage	Characteristics	Example of what a child can do
		Topic 1: Relative density
		Topic 2: Oxidation and reduction
Preoperational 1	Pupils: • Offer inconsistent observations • Treat each object one by one and are unable to group into classes (will change the class of an object to meet the immediate circumstances) • Tend to be egocentric and impute 'will' to the objects	
Early concrete operations	Pupils: • Can place observations or objects into groups • Can perceive and use two variable causal relationships • Have a sense of number • Can order a series of objects	Can place objects in two (or three) groups: things that float in water, things that sink (and things that sink when pushed). Pure oxygen makes things burn more brightly than air itself.
Mature concrete operations	Pupils: • Can mentally model across categories (see, for example, heavy and light objects that can float and sink) • Are unable to explain observations that require imagined or abstract concepts • Can use reverse reasoning (e.g. acids make litmus turn red, therefore anything that turns litmus red is an acid) • Are unable to imagine all the possible variables in a situation, therefore are unable to design an experiment where all the variables are well controlled • Can follow stepwise instructions for a practical but may have no overview of what it is all about	Understands that you can have big things that are heavy and big things that are light but still cannot find an adequate explanation for why some things sink and some things float in water. Carbon can reduce metal oxides to the metal. Oxygen can oxidize a metal. Metals can be placed in a reactivity series by their speed and vigour of burning.

Stage	Characteristics	Example of what a child can do
		Topic 1: Relative density
		Topic 2: Oxidation and reduction
Early formal operations	Pupils: • Can hold a number of variables in mind at once and see how they may be related to one another • Can offer the beginning of explanatory thinking, therefore can use the particle model to explain properties of solids, liquids and gases	Rejects hypothesis that buoyancy is determined either by volume alone or by size alone. Understands the need to consider mass of a given volume of stuff. Buoyancy depends on mass/volume.
		Has a model of a chemical reaction conserving the elements so can predict that when carbon or a reactive metal (M) reduces an oxide, CO_2 or MO must be produced. Can deduce a reactivity series and can use the series to make predictions.
Mature formal	Pupils: • Can use theoretical models and have the ability to generate hypotheses and ability to generate hypotheses and design experiments to test them	Understands the complete relationship – floating and sinking depends on the density of the solid relative to the density of the liquid.
		Appreciates that there are different theories or models of oxidation/reduction and can critically compare them. Can use a model of a reaction even when what they see is paradoxical, e.g. magnesium burning in steam (able to deduce that gas produced must be hydrogen).

Figure 2.3 *Characteristics of the Piagetian stages of development* (Adey, 1993)

further insight into pupils' learning through his study of the role that people working together play in mutual cognitive development (Vygotsky, 1978). When pupils are trying to solve problems that require a greater understanding than they currently hold, they can make progress in three possible ways. They can think hard about their partially formed ideas and see how they fit in with their established understanding and come up with a solution by themselves. They could work with others (teachers or pupils) and learn by talking about the meanings of scientific concepts and arguing over what constitutes a good explanation for the problem they are working on. Or they could simply come up with the answer by chance (Figure 2.5). Vygotsky proposed a model of learning

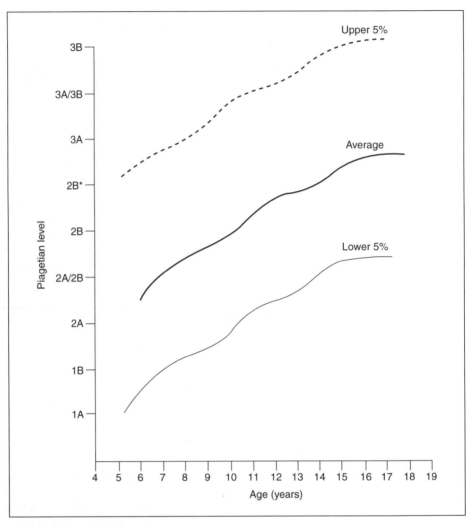

Figure 2.4 *A representation in Piagetian terms of boys' development during their time at school*

involving two 'layers': an inner layer consisting of the learning that an individual can achieve independently, and an outer layer that requires the help of adults or more capable peers. He called the distance between these two layers the Zone of Proximal Development (ZPD). Vygotsky argued that intelligence is determined not only by a capacity to learn but also by a capacity for being taught.

In a group situation there will be interactions between the ZPDs of all the members of the group. Vygotsky saw the ZPD lying not simply in an individual's own mind but in the shared space that is created during the social interaction. In such a situation Pupil A can learn from pupil B by an input that affects his partially formed ideas. But pupil A can also learn from pupil B's partially formed ideas. They are effectively feeding off one another's different levels of understanding.

Bruner took Vygotsky's ideas further and introduced the concept of 'scaffold-

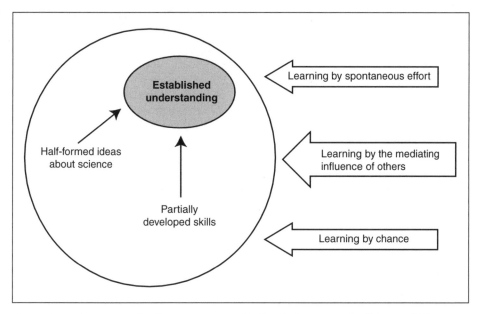

Figure 2.5 *Three sets of influences on pupils that help to turn half-formed ideas into new established knowledge*

ing' (Bruner, 1986). This involves the teacher setting up a support structure to help the learner keep on the right track and avoid too many pitfalls. The teacher's job is to stimulate and support learning while promoting independence through activity, questioning, explanation and discussion.

Bruner also pointed out that humans have the capacity to invent tools to enhance their existing capabilities. Through time, learning has been enhanced by the introduction of many educational tools such as those associated with writing and publishing, the ability to represent ideas symbolically, a whole range of developments in communications technology and through the use of ICT. Although scaffolding has traditionally been associated with support by the intervention of another human being, support can also be provided by a computer. For example, when drawing graphs of experimental data the computer can reduce the cognitive load on the pupil by taking care of the mechanical aspects and thereby give more 'space' for the pupil to focus on the conclusions from the data (Kennewell *et al.*, 2000).

6 HELPING PUPILS TO LEARN: EVERYDAY EXAMPLES

So far we have been mainly looking at theories about how pupils' learn. In the remaining sections of this chapter we will look at how these impinge on classroom practice. Oh, and there will be a little more theory just in case you were missing it.

What follows is a brief look at the factors you need to take into account when planning all your lessons. You need to read this in conjunction with the section on planning in Chapter 3 (see p. 39).

6.1 Your knowledge

It probably goes without saying that you should make sure that you are completely familiar with the subject matter before you go into the lesson, but I have seen far too many students become unstuck in a lesson when they have thought it sufficient just to read through the double page of the textbook used by the pupils. You need to feel confident that you know what you are talking about and the pupils need to have confidence in you. This can be a particular problem with new teachers and more able pupils who may deliberately not learn something until they have checked out its accuracy with another person.

6.2 Appreciate pupils' prior learning

In order to avoid pupils becoming bored and disaffected you need to avoid repetition of work. You should find out what topics have been covered and what types of experiences pupils have had earlier on in the school and at primary school. You need to also be aware of what they have done in other subjects, e.g. environmental work in geography, materials in D&T, the development of an aspect of science in history. However, not all learning takes place in school: pupils learn a lot through their daily experiences and this can have a significant effect on their understanding of science as is shown in the section on CLIS below.

6.3 Understand the conceptual demand of the topic

There is a danger here in the interpretation of Piaget's work. You may look at the topic you are about to teach a class and deduce that the work has a cognitive demand beyond the capabilities of your class. Do you carry on believing that they are not going to understand and curse the 'idiot' that insisted that it should be in the curriculum at KS3? Or do you think of ways of breaking it down, look for analogies that might help and be prepared to come back to it at a later date? There are no hard and fast rules to the learning game and you may find it possible to move pupils through quite difficult hurdles by providing the right sort of scaffolding. That's what good teaching is all about.

6.4 Making the lesson objectives explicit

We cannot expect pupils to learn in some sort of haphazard manner: they need to be directed in their learning to avoid the risk of them missing the key points in the lesson. You can do this by giving a few, clear introductory remarks at the start of the lesson together with an outline of the objectives on the board. These may not be in the form that you would write down in your lesson plan as they need to be in a form of language that would appeal to the pupils and can be easily understood. For example, you could say: 'What we are going to do today is to find out what factors affect . . .?' or 'We are going to find out the relationship between . . . and . . .' Alternatively, you can try to get the pupils to tell you what they think the objectives are going to be. First you would give them a brief introduction about the type of work they are going to do and then ask the question 'What do you think I want you to learn this lesson?'

6.5 Linking to previous work

You need to help pupils make the link between the present work and things they have done in the past by doing a little revision or by asking the pupils to try to make the connections: 'What does this remind you of?'; 'Last term we did some work on . . . What do you think the connection is with what we are doing now?' You may try to get across to pupils that you are trying to build up a big picture of science and as they go through school more parts will be added to the picture. Some parts may need revisiting as we find out that the parts we had weren't quite good enough.

6.6 Motivating the pupils to learn

Sometimes this can be the most difficult part of a teacher's job. Pupils can be reluctant to participate in your lesson for a whole host of reasons, many of which are concerned with their lives outside the classroom. What you have to do is to convince them that learning is valuable and that learning about science is not only interesting but can be fun. You may find that many pupils become turned off science if it is presented in an abstract way with the emphasis on learning about processes and facts. Telling pupils that they have to learn it because it will be in the exam might motivate some but it will have no impression on those who are disaffected. A good teacher is one who can capture the hearts and minds of his/her pupils and develop in them a desire to learn. This will happen when they feel good about the lesson. They know that the teacher will have prepared something interesting for them to do. She/he will make them feel good about themselves through encouragement and praising them for making an effort. She/he will show an interest in them as individuals and talk to them at various stages of the lesson. Even a simple question such as 'How are you doing today, Jo?' can spark off a feeling of being wanted and generate some enthusiasm for learning. Abraham Maslow has produced a model for motivation based on a hierarchy of human needs (Figure 2.6). The higher levels bear out what was said in the previous paragraph about the importance of giving attention to individuals and praise for effort and attainment. But it is also important not to forget the lowest levels. Pupils are not going to learn if they are hungry or in a classroom that is either too cold or too hot. To some extent this is out of your control, but you need to keep a look out for pupils' eating habits and monitor the temperature of your classroom.

6.7 Breaking down the work into suitably sized chunks of learning

So far we have only talked about pupils' understanding from the point of view of the conceptual difficulty of the topic. You could think of this in terms of the depth of understanding. What we are going to look at now is breadth of understanding and the retention of the knowledge. A useful model for thinking

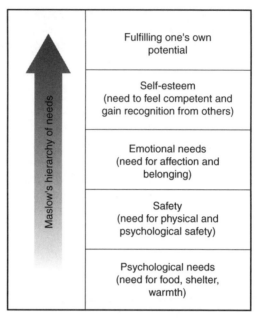

Figure 2.6 *Influences on motivation based on satisfying basic human needs* (Maslow, 1987)

about how we remember things is to consider the three separate stages of learning (The Learners' Cooperative, 1998):

- the sensory register (alerting the brain of the new information);
- the working memory (the initial 'digestion' of the information);
- the long term memory (retention of the information).

Figure 2.7 shows the key features of each level of memory based on the work of a number of research psychologists. There are a number of important messages

Memory system	Sensory registry	Working memory	Long term memory
Definition	Where attention is grabbed	Where conscious thinking happens	Where information is stored
Operating time	Less than a second	About seven minutes	A long time
Influenced by	• Mood • Mental state • External stimuli	• The size of the information 'chunk' • What the learner knows already	• Use of the information • Revision and review

Figure 2.7 *Levels of memory*

http://www.rtweb.info

that this research has for teachers. First, it emphasises the importance of creating the right sort of atmosphere for learning. The build up to the learning may take 5–10 minutes but the actual learning interlude will be very small indeed. You might also say that it provides support for repeating key points on the basis that if it didn't hit the target first time round, keep shooting until you do. Secondly, the research shows us that learners process chunks of information in the working memory. The question is, how big is a chunk? If the chunks are too small then the learner may have difficulty in joining all the parts together to make the whole. If the chunks are too large the learner finds it impossible to manipulate the information. As a teacher you will have to decide about breaking information down into suitably-sized chunks. The third point to note is the importance of revisiting and revising previously learnt science. This can be done by deliberately referring back to previous work whenever there is a connection to be made or by periodically holding review sessions ('What have we learnt in this [topic, month, term, year, etc.]?').

6.8   Making science sexy

Pupils aren't going to learn science just because it is an important subject. They are likely to learn science if they see it as a vibrant, interesting subject that has something to offer them. Somehow or other you need to get across to pupils that science is exciting and worthwhile. You can do a lot towards this by creating a positive atmosphere for science through the layout of your room, the way in which you present information and your approach to teaching in general, as illustrated by the points in Figure 2.8. Show them that you love your subject and you will be surprised how quickly your enthusiasm will rub off.

Practical activity 2.3

Bearing in mind the information in Figure 2.7 analyse one of your lessons by answering the following questions:

- At what points in the lesson did the pupils 'receive' the new information they were required to learn?
- What did you do to make sure they were receptive to that new information?
- How did you break it down into suitably-sized chunks?
- To what extent did you call on the pupils' long-term memory?

7   HELPING PUPILS TO LEARN: THE CLIS APPROACH

The Children's Learning in Science Project (CLIS project or CLISP) was concerned with finding out about pupils' understanding about a range of scientific phenomena contained in the National Curriculum. Rosalind Driver and her co-workers at the University of Leeds directed the project during the 1980s, working on such fundamental ideas as heat, the particle theory of matter, light, nutrition,

Room	Audio-visual aids	Teacher talk
• Tidy and uncluttered • Walls covered with posters produced by pupils (renewed regularly) • Graffiti free	• Clear OHTs (not too much writing, large font-size – 18+) • Use of modern technology and up to date videos and software whenever possible	• Clear and at a level appropriate to the age and ability of the class • Broken down into suitably sized chunks • Positive and upbeat
Tone of the lesson	**Activities**	**Imagery**
• Encouraging – plenty of praise for making an effort, correct answers, good work • Creating an atmosphere where pupils are not afraid to ask questions	• Varied, meeting the needs of the different types of learners • Sufficiently challenging to help the pupils to move on intellectually	• Clear anologies • Use of models • Inviting pupils to use their imagination
Classroom control	**Classroom management**	
• Pupils are aware of the rules and know the consequences if they are broken • The teacher is on the ball – eyes and ears are everywhere • At the first sign of disruption the teacher takes appropriate action	• Organizing the pupils into suitable learning groups • Keeping the pupils on task • Making sure that a suitable amount of time is allotted for each task • Clear transitions between tasks	

Figure 2.8 *Creating the right sort of atmosphere for learning to take place*

energy and chemical reactions. This work, and the work of other science educators from around the world, gave rise to a considerable amount of data about how pupils interpreted the world in which they lived. A substantial amount of this work has now been summarized and put into a form that is easy to access (see e.g. Driver *et al.*, 1994a, 1994b; Barker, 2000).

Some ideas that pupils' hold match with the accepted views of science but pupils will also hold a large number of misconceptions. You have to remember that quite a lot of science is contrary to what you might expect. For example, you might think that if you fired a bullet from a gun horizontally and at the same time dropped a bullet from the same height, that the dropped one would reach the ground first. However, this is not true: the laws of physics tell us that they both hit the ground at the same time, and this is what happens in reality. When pupils are asked where wood comes from they don't immediately turn to their knowledge of photosynthesis and the understanding that carbohydrates are formed from carbon dioxide and water, they tend to go for what seems like the commonsense idea that the solid wood is made from the equally substantial soil.

It's not just pupils that have misconceptions about science – many adults and even new teachers sometimes don't quite get it right. Many pupils' understandings are firmly held and make sense to them. They have probably been built up over a period of time through everyday experiences and the interactions with a lot of different people. For example, an explanation that a parent or other significant adult gives a child at an early stage in his/her development can have a lasting effect because of the relationship between the adult and the child. The type of learning where pupils construct their ideas over time is referred to as 'constructivism'. The first thing you need to do is to recognize that pupils come to your lessons with alternative understandings (sometimes referred to as alternative frameworks) of science. Then you need to ask yourself what you are going to do about it? The response might be that you are going to teach them the correct science accompanied by a few demonstrations to illustrate the phenomena. Well, that may work and the pupils may be able to answer examination questions on the topic but all the research indicates that pupils will still retain their alternative frameworks. Don't take my word for it, ask a fellow PGCE student to tell you how a tree grows, or what happens to the current in a simple electric circuit. These students will have at least a grade C in GCSE science but I would be surprised if you get many correct answers. So we can train pupils to jump through the hoops but perhaps, in the main, we are failing to instil real understanding and long-term learning. If pupils are to move towards a correct understanding of the phenomena they need to go through a series of stages that prompt them to reflect on their present ideas and recognize that their explanations do not hold up to thorough cross-examination.

Following on from an introduction to the topic the first major stage in what is called a constructivist approach to teaching would be for the teacher to get pupils to make explicit their present understanding about the topic. This would be followed by a series of strategies (Figure 2.9) to raise the pupils' awareness of alternative viewpoints and to get the pupils to critically examine their own understanding. This would be followed by the elimination of some of the alternative frameworks due to the fact that they don't hold up to scrutiny. Pupils are then presented with new experiences and asked to explain these in terms of newly-constructed ideas. This application, together with the success it brings in terms of being able to explain phenomena, plays a large part in establishing the correct science but is still not enough. The pupils need to go on to review their

Practical activity 2.4

Devise a short test, say between one and four questions, on a topic you are about to teach. The questions should be taken from everyday events (to provide familiarity) and should ask pupils to give you an explanation in terms of the science that they know. A cartoon picture for each question might help to promote interest. For example, you could have a picture of some youngsters kicking a football and ask the following: 'A football was blown up so that it was hard for the game. It was then left overnight and first thing in the morning it was found to be much softer. The ball didn't leak. Explain why it went soft overnight (in terms of your knowledge about particles)'. You will find lots of examples of this type of question in the literature on misconceptions.

Orientation

- Use of stimulus material, e.g. newspaper items, demonstrations, discussion of everyday events
- Preparatory homework, e.g. asking pupils to write down what they already know about the topic, carrying out an experiment or survey at home

↓

Elicitation of ideas

- Whole class and/or group discussion followed by reporting back
- Ideas compiled on the board, OHP or flip chart (in a place where they can be kept for referral later on)
- Practical activity followed by class discussion

↓

Restructuring of ideas

A process of clarifying ideas through group and class discussion

↓

Getting pupils to question their original ideas by exposing them to cognitive conflict situations e.g. through teacher demonstrations, personal experiments, worksheets

↓

Constructing new ideas through activities such as teacher input, reading, discussion

↓

Testing out the newly constructed ideas through activities such as: practical work, teacher demonstration

↓

Application of ideas

- Opportunities to use the ideas in problem solving situations
- Writing about the science in their own words
- Carrying out experiments and interpeting them

↓

Review

- Preparing posters summarizing the key points
- Personal writing
- Discussion sessions

Figure 2.9 *Key phases in teaching from a constructivist standpoint* (adapted from Needham, 1987)

ideas and, from time to time, come back to them to check that they still work. It's a long process, but then deep learning is going to take a long time.

8 HELPING PUPILS TO LEARN: AN INTERVENTION PROGRAMME

We have seen from the work of Adey and Shayer described above that a considerable proportion of the school population work at the level of concrete operations throughout their school life, whereas the science they are taught requires them to function at the formal level of thinking. In order to help pupils improve their ability to think, Adey, Shayer and Yates (1989) devised a series of activities that pupils can perform during KS3 which have been derived from the research project called Cognitive Acceleration through Science Education (CASE). The activities can be carried out over a period of time while the pupils are following a 'normal' science course. They are content-free and the process is described as an intervention approach rather than instruction in science. In addition to the set of pupils' materials, collectively called 'Thinking Science', there is an in-service training (INSET) handbook that takes teachers through the procedures that need to be followed to teach CASE (Adey, 1993). The themes of the activities in the pupils' pack are: control of variables, proportionality, probability, compensation and equilibrium, combinations, correlation, classification, formal models and compound variables. The activities are based around a set of clearly defined principles sometimes referred to as the Five Pillars of (CASE) Wisdom. These are:

1. *Concrete preparation*
   Based on the work of Piaget and Vygotsky, pupils are presented with situations that they are relatively familiar with but the tasks they are asked to do have a high cognitive demand.

2. *Cognitive conflict*
   The nature of the task is such that pupils cannot solve the problem using their present level of thinking.

3. *Construction*
   The purpose of the cognitive conflict is to put the pupils in a situation where they have to construct new reasoning patterns in order to solve the problem. With Thinking Science it is not just the understanding of the concepts that is constructed but, more importantly, the reasoning patterns of formal operations.

4. *Metacognition*
   This is the process of getting pupils to become more conscious of their own thinking, to the extent they will reflect back on a problem and consider how it was solved and what the difficulties were.

5. *Bridging*
   CASE activities are planned to raise pupils' overall thinking skills, not just their ability to function more effectively in science. The process of bridging involves pupils being able to take a principle or idea from the context in which it was developed and apply it to a new situation.

An increasing number of schools are using the CASE materials in the hope that they will help pupils to understand science and be able to deal with the increasing complexity of science as they move on to KS4 work. The original research reported that not only did the use of CASE materials have an impact on pupils' immediate thinking but also it had long-term effects resulting in 'CASE pupils' doing better at GCSE than comparable pupils who had not followed the intervention programme. There is also plenty of anecdotal evidence from teachers saying that 'CASE pupils' are better at tackling investigations.

Practical activity 2.5

Look at a series of lessons you have planned for the teaching of a topic and identify the key concepts that are going to be taught.

How many of these will involve the pupils having to accept what you tell them?

Are there any opportunities for you to introduce cognitive conflict situations? If there are, you will find it useful to try these out and to evaluate the effect on pupils' thinking.

Are there any ideas or principles that can be used in future topics?

CONCLUSION

Your role as a teacher is to provide opportunities for pupils to learn. Learning is going to be more effective when:

- the pupils are actively involved in the learning situation rather than as passive bystanders;
- the pupils know exactly what it is they are supposed to learn;
- the teacher provides materials and teaching situations that cater for the individual differences amongst the learners;
- the teacher structures the lesson to provide clear explanations and support;
- the teacher is aware of pupils' prior understanding;
- the teacher provides suitable motivation for the pupils;
- pupils take responsibility for their own learning.

CHAPTER 3

Planning your teaching

INTRODUCTION

There is no one correct formula for producing a good lesson, so much depends on the subject matter and the pupils you are teaching. However, good lessons don't just happen by chance, they require careful planning and preparation. The first stage is to familiarize yourself with what it is you are required to teach and the best way of doing this is to read the Science National Curriculum. This will give you a brief outline of the content together with some guidance on the teaching approach. You then need to take a look at how the national curriculum is interpreted by different textbooks and the teachers in your school. Then, hopefully, you will be in a position to start planning lessons of your own.

By the end of this chapter you should:

- understand the purpose of the Science National Curriculum and be able to use it to plan lessons;
- appreciate the value of observing other teachers and know about strategies for learning from these experiences;
- understand the structure of lessons and know how to plan for various activities;
- understand the importance of having clear learning outcomes for the lesson;
- know how to plan a series of lessons and develop a scheme of work.

1   THE CURRICULUM

The curriculum is a term used to describe, in outline, all that pupils are taught or experience during their period of education. This includes the subjects that pupils are taught (the subject curriculum); the curriculum concerned with personal and social development (the pastoral curriculum); the activities that take place out of main line teaching (the extra-curricular curriculum); and the way in which the school helps pupils to develop attitudes, values and relationships (the hidden curriculum). So where does the National Curriculum (NC) fit into the picture? The National Curriculum is the statutory part of the whole curriculum and it is divided up into nine subject curricular and aspects of the pastoral curriculum (DfEE and QCA, 1999).

2 | THE SCIENCE NATIONAL CURRICULUM

The Science National Curriculum is important because it describes what must be taught in all state schools from the age of 5 to 16. The situation is complicated by the fact that England, Wales and Northern Ireland have slightly different national curricular in terms of content and emphasis. In addition to outlining what topics are to be taught, the NC document describes the system of assessment to be used at key stages 1–3. At key stage 4, the GCSE grading system takes over as the method of assessment (see Chapter 8). The content of the NC is called the Programme of Study (PoS) and for each key stage (KS) it is divided into four parts:

- Scientific Enquiry
- Life Processes and Living Things
- Materials and their Properties
- Physical Processes.

The last three of these headings are virtually self explanatory, covering biological sciences, chemical and Earth sciences, and physical science respectively. The Scientific Enquiry sections identify aspects of teaching and learning that should be mapped onto the content of the other three programmes of study. The Scientific Enquiry PoS indicates how the science should be presented to pupils. In particular, it looks at what pupils should know about the way scientific knowledge is constructed and how pupils should go about investigating a situation themselves. In the Welsh NC emphasis is given to the communication of science and the use of correct terms, symbols and conventions.

The level descriptions give an indication of pupil achievement in terms of the expected outcomes of the programme of study. These level descriptions are called Attainment Targets and there are four sets of them to match the four parts of the programme of study. Each Attainment Target contains descriptions of pupils' performance at eight levels and a further description for very able pupils called Exceptional Performance. The purpose of these descriptions is to help teachers gauge the achievement of pupils at the end of a key stage using a scale that is common across the country. Some teachers go beyond this and use the descriptions to grade some of the important pieces of work completed during the key stage. The appropriate way of using the description is to see which paragraph best matches the performance of the pupil. The teacher would then look at the descriptions for the levels above and below to confirm that the best fit level had been chosen. You need to bear in mind that the descriptions are not criteria and it is not necessary for a pupil to satisfy all the statements given in order to be awarded a particular level.

In addition to helping pupils gain an understanding of science, the National Curriculum identifies opportunities for pupils to develop skills that go beyond the boundaries of the science curriculum. These are presented differently in the National Curriculum documents of England and Wales but the underlying common principles apply to both. The key skills (common requirements in Wales) are aspects of learning that will help pupils to improve their performance in education, work and life in general. At key stages 3 and 4 there is no formal assessment of these skills but pupils who continue their study beyond the age of 16 will have the opportunity to work towards key skills qualifications (see Chapter 8). The six key skills are:

1. *Communication*
   This includes speaking, reading and writing, and examples include: presenting information graphically, writing about science for different audiences, presenting their ideas to groups of people.

2. *Application of number* (mathematical skills in Wales)
   This requires the pupils to develop the understanding and use of mathematical language in order to carry out calculations and process data. There are many opportunities in science for pupils to carry out calculations and for some pupils this is one of the most challenging areas of the subject.

3. *Information technology*
   This is about using IT to locate, analyse and present information. It is about when and how to use IT for maximum benefit. For example, pupils can use computers to log data from appropriate experiments, sort data using a spreadsheet, and locate information on websites.

4. *Working with others* (part of Personal and Social Education in Wales)
   Pupils frequently work together in science lessons during practical work and group discussions. These give rise to opportunities for pupils to work together to achieve a common goal, supporting one another and sharing the available resources.

5. *Improving own learning and performance* (part of Personal and Social Education in Wales)
   This is about helping pupils to become more responsible for their own learning through a process of target setting, reflection and planning for improvement. Pupils need to be able to learn from a variety of sources in addition to the teacher and gain an appreciation that work needs to be completed by the deadline.

6. *Problem solving*
   A lot of science is about solving problems and this aspect of the NC gives rise to opportunities for pupils to use the knowledge and skills that they have gained to tackle problems.

In addition, the NC in Wales identifies two other skills that should be developed through the teaching of science, Curriculum Cymreig (incorporating the cultural, economic, environmental, historical and linguistic characteristics of Wales) and Creative Skills (providing opportunities for pupils to express their ideas and use their imagination).

Information about the National Curriculum can be obtained from the following websites:

- *www.nc.uk.net/*
- *www.accac.org.uk/english.html*

Practical activity 3.1

Take a small section of the National Curriculum, e.g. Section 1.2 from Life Processes and Living Things: 'The functions of the cell membrane, cytoplasm and nucleus in plant and animal cells', and examine how this is interpreted by looking at two or three KS3 textbooks. Identify what the pupils will have learnt by the end of the lesson and list the type of pupil activities carried out in the lesson (see Figure 3.7 for some examples).

3   LEARNING FROM OTHER TEACHERS

The best way of learning about how the NC is implemented is to talk to experienced teachers and observe them in the classroom. Through observation you can learn a great deal about the art of teaching and you will find it worthwhile not to restrict your observation to science but to spend some time watching other subjects being taught. The skills of carrying out group-work, questioning pupils, controlling pupils' behaviour, etc., are common to all subjects and you may find that the 'school expert' in one particular area is not a scientist. You are in a very privileged position when observing someone teach and it goes without saying that you should be courteous and polite. You may be surprised to find that even experienced teachers find it a nerve-racking experience to be observed by someone and may be considerably irritated if you say or do something that is inappropriate. Check that you know what your role in the lesson is going to be by talking to the teacher before the lesson. For example, you would find it useful to:

- ask the teacher if it is ok to make a few notes;
- inform the teacher that you are focusing on one or two particular aspects of teaching during the lesson in order to improve your own technique;
- ask what you should do when the pupils are carrying out practical work or a similar task;
- ask what you should do if you see a pupil misbehaving (if you haven't cleared this with the teacher and you tell a pupil off, the teacher may think that his/ her discipline has been undermined);
- ask the teacher if you can talk to him/her after the lesson (the teacher may not be able to talk to you directly after the lesson but you should be able to find a mutually acceptable time. This meeting will give you the opportunity to ask the teacher why he/she did certain things. Don't expect an answer every time, sometimes it is difficult to know why we do things in certain ways).

You are strongly advised to concentrate on one or two aspects of teaching in any one lesson otherwise you will find it difficult to analyse exactly what is going on. At the start of your school experience you will find it valuable to concentrate on looking at the structure of the lesson and how the teacher organizes the movement from one episode to another. You may find it useful to use an observation schedule, as illustrated in Figure 3.1. On the right-hand side you

Class   No. of pupils: Ability grouping: Period: Date:

Topic:

1.   Entry and setting down: gaining attention
How is the entry managed? What do the pupils do? Teacher actions? How does the teacher gain the class's attention?

Time:

2.   Lesson beginning
To what extent does the teacher recap on previous work? How does the teacher introduce the topic? How does the teacher convey the aims of the lesson to the pupils? How does the teacher find out about pupils' prior knowledge of the topic?

Time:

3.   Main activities
Identify the main activities, noting the time spent on each and how the teacher moves the pupils from one activity to another.

Teacher activity	Pupil activity	Time

4.   Lesson ending
What happens – summary, packing away of resources, reference to original aims, questioning, etc.?

Time:

5.   Dismissal procedure
How is this organized? Specific routines?

Time:

Figure 3.1 *An observation schedule to study the different phases of a lesson* (adapted from Parkinson and Roe, 1997, p. 375)

could keep a rolling check on the lapsed time in order to help you make judgements as to how long to spend on particular tasks.

Sometimes it is best to carry out your observation sitting at a suitable place in the room but on other occasions you will find it beneficial to move around the laboratory and interact with the pupils. You may not see everything that is going on but by talking to the pupils you will gain an insight into their thinking about the lesson. You can devise your own form for monitoring what goes on which should allow you to keep a separate check on pupil and teacher activity and the time spent on particular tasks.

It is interesting to observe the same teacher teaching different classes and watch how his/her teaching style changes depending on factors such as the age and ability of the pupils, his/her relationship with the class, or the nature of the topic being taught. In certain circumstances the teacher will want to dictate everything that goes on in the room giving very little latitude to the pupils. In other circumstances the teacher may be prepared to ease back and allow the pupils more freedom as long as the lesson keeps within the defined limits of the lesson plan.

You will probably find that initially you will adopt one style with all your classes, but as your confidence grows and you get to know the children in your classes you will be able to switch styles to match different situations. For more information on teaching styles see Capel *et al.* (1995, p. 249) or Pollard and Triggs (1997, p. 262)

Practical activity 3.2

During an observation lesson, use the list of points below to help you to analyse how a teacher controls the behaviour of his/her pupils.

1. General demeanour
   Does the teacher look calm? Is s/he rushing around trying to get things ready or does s/he delegate tasks? In what ways does the teacher use body language to control the class?

2. Minor breaches of indiscipline
   How does the teacher deal with pupils chewing gum in the class? What happens when pupils talk out of turn? How does the teacher deal with pupils who are not paying attention?

3. Preventing discipline problems
   Identify aspects of the lesson where the teacher has planned for the pupils to do something with the intent of reducing the opportunity for them to become disruptive e.g. the they are constantly on task and have little 'free' time. How does the teacher calm potentially disruptive situations?

4. Dealing with more major problems
   How does the teacher scale up the punishment? How does the teacher deal with particularly bad cases of disruption?

Also see Practical activity 4.3 and Parkinson (1994, pp. 54–6) for further ideas on observing teachers.

4 PLANNING YOUR LESSONS

In the time normally allocated for a science lesson (about one hour) you are faced with a number of challenges, from maintaining order to generating enthusiasm for the topic and getting them to learn something new. Quite a tall order, particularly as you are likely to be working with a group of young people of varying academic ability and willingness to learn. It is vitally important that you are clear about what you and the pupils are going to be doing during the lesson and that both you and the pupils know what the outcomes of the lesson are going to be. There is no fixed answer as to how long a lesson plan should be or the level of detail it should contain but it is worth spending a few moments reflecting on its purposes before you start to write. The prime purpose of the plan is to help you to organize your thoughts on what should happen in the lesson and, as such, it is a personal document and can contain squiggles and hieroglyphs that only you can understand. Lesson plans are also of use in helping you to analyse and evaluate your teaching and can be used as a framework for making judgements on your performance and planning for improvement. In addition, they serve as a record, so that in future years you can look back and see how you organized the teaching of certain topics or planned a particular practical. Another important use of lesson plans is as evidence of the quality of your planning over a period of time for assessment purposes on your ITE course.

The layouts given in Figures 3.2 and 3.3 illustrate different ways of structuring your lesson plan. There are, of course, many other formats for lesson plans but you should make sure that whichever system you choose must be clear so that it is easy to refer to during the lesson. You may find that you have a memory lapse and need to know what happens next. Therefore, you need to avoid dense script and go for short phrases or paragraphs using a highlighter to identify key points – but be careful not to overdo this as it will quickly defeat the object of making things easy to see. Many students, particularly in the early stages of their course, want to write down key parts of the lesson in detail or write notes on the topic to help them learn the science. It is a good idea to keep these separate from the main plan but in easy reach, if only to boost your confidence.

The objectives are a very important part of the plan. They represent the key things that you want the pupils to learn by the end of the lesson and, as such, need to be written in very clear and precise terms. When writing the objectives it is worthwhile spending some time thinking about how you are going to be able to check to see if the objectives have been met. If one of your objectives is that pupils should enjoy carrying out a particular experiment, then you need to think how you are going to structure the practical so that they do enjoy it, and how you might check their level of enjoyment. In this case, it could simply be observation of the pupils during the practical accompanied by a few questions to groups and individuals. Your objectives will generally fall into one of three categories:

- cognitive – pupils should know (be able to recall); pupils should understand; pupils should be able to describe; pupils should be able to calculate;
- affective – pupils should appreciate; pupils should be creative; pupils should use their imagination; pupils should enjoy;
- skills – pupils should be able to measure; pupils should be able to communicate; pupils should be able to observe.

Lesson Plan	*Title of the topic:*
Date:	
Room:	
Time:	*You need to know when the lesson starts and ends.*
Class:	*Remind yourself about the age and ability grouping of the pupils.*

SOW reference: *This section could also contain cross links to textbooks.*

NC reference:

Objectives: Pupils should know that

   •

Pupils should understand

   •

Pupils should be able to

   •

Resources:

Time	**Teacher activity**	**Pupil activity**
Break up the lesson into 5, 10 or 15 minutes episodes.	*Check that the activities in these two columns will enable the pupils to meet the objectives stated above.*	*This column helps to focus your attention on what the pupils are learning.*

Safety   *What risks are you and the pupils going to be exposed to during the lesson? Consult the relevant safety publications.*

Figure 3.2 *Outline of a lesson plan (1)*

LESSON PLAN:

Class: Date: Day: Period: Room: No. of pupils: Set:

Objectives	List what you want the pupils to achieve by the end of the lesson.
Key words	List important words that you want pupils to use during the lesson and understand by the end of the lesson.

Timings	Focus	Teacher activity	Student activity	Resources
Give approximate timings.	List the type of activity being carried out.	Indicate what you will be doing.	Indicate what the pupils will be doing.	Briefly list the resources being used.

Homework tasks and deadline	Remind yourself of the homework you are going to set and when you want it in.
Differentiation	Include any special things you will do for pupils of different abilities.
Assessment	Briefly indicate how you are going to check pupils' understanding during the lesson.
NC reference	Keep a check that you are covering the National Curriculum.
Issues	A reminder of other key things, e.g. names of pupils who behaved badly last lesson, safety precautions that you need to take, names of pupils who have to leave early for music lessons.

Figure 3.3 *Outline of a lesson plan (2)*

Objectives where the outcome can be observed		
By the end of the lesson pupils should be able to:		
list	describe	compare
identify	name	explain
select	demonstrate the ability to	discuss
solve	demonstrate the understanding of	sequence
Objectives focused on pupils' development		
By the end of the lesson pupils will:		
be aware of	have an understanding of	been introduced to
have considered	gained increased insight into	begun to analyse
developed the ability to	improved performance in	have had practice in

Figure 3.4 *Phrases that are used to write objectives*

A characteristic of a poor lesson is that it does not have clearly stated objectives. You may find it useful to use very specific language when writing your objectives to ensure that you have clear learning targets for the lesson. Figure 3.4 gives a number of examples of the types of phrase you could use.

Practical activity 3.3

Reviewing objectives. Comment on the value of the following lesson objectives:

- Pupils should be able to list the characteristics of living things.
- Pupils should be familiar with the working of the muscles in the human arm.
- Pupils should be able to select the apparatus for carrying out the investigation.
- Pupils should know whether animals are alive or not.
- Pupils should learn how to behave.
- Pupils should know that the current splits at junctions in a parallel circuit.
- Pupils should be able to work in groups.
- Pupils should understand the principles of a series/parallel circuit.

Discuss your responses with your mentor.

In order to make sure that the lesson content matches the needs of the pupils you will have to carry out some research to find out about the range of ability of the pupils in the class and what work they have done before. You also need to have a clear picture of the concepts involved in the topic and how they relate to ideas covered in other topics. There are several ways of doing this and you will find it worthwhile to spend some time on each. The first thing to do is to construct a concept map (see p. 77) showing the relationship between the key ideas. This will help you to clarify the links between the ideas and identify aspects of the work that you don't completely understand. Second, it is worthwhile looking at the common misconceptions held by pupils. Driver *et al.* (1994a, 1994b) have compiled a book outlining the research evidence of children's ideas on a wide range of National Curriculum topics and have produced learning maps showing how teachers can structure their work to enable children to work towards a correct understanding. Third, you should look at how the topic is structured in a textbook or one of the books specifically written for new science teachers (Jerram, 1999; McDuell, 2000; Reiss, 1999; Sang, 2000a; Wilson, 1999; Winterbottom, 1999).

Once you are happy with the content you need to ensure that you are confident about the skills that both you and the pupils will need to have in order to make the lesson a success. In some cases these may need signposting up to the pupils several lessons in advance. For example, you may want them to draw a graph of their experimental results and in order to prepare them you may give them a homework task on graph plotting and interpreting graphs.

You will find it helpful to break up the lesson into a series of linked episodes each serving a particular function. The minimum number will be three (the start, the middle and the end) but frequently you will want to break it up into smaller units of time to ensure that the lesson contains a variety of activities. Figure 3.5 illustrates some of the components that could be included in the different episodes of a lesson and these are explained in more detail in the sections that follow.

Some students think that lesson planning is just about filling in a form to keep

Practical activity 3.4

Find out the common misconceptions held by pupils for a topic you are about to teach and write them down.

Check that you understand the concept correctly. Don't be embarrassed, even people with a degree in science may not understand some fundamental ideas correctly.

What does the list of misconceptions tell you about the teaching of this topic?

How will you use the knowledge that some pupils hold these ideas when you plan your lesson?

Read the section on starter activities in the KS3 National Science Strategy Formwork document. How do these activities deal with pupils' misconceptions?

Starting the lesson

- Whenever possible be at the room before the pupils
- If possible have a word with them in the corridor
- Talk to pupils as they enter the room
- Instruct pupils to get bags and coats away and books and pens out
- Get everyone's attention to start the lesson

Getting the brains in gear

- Let the pupils know what they are going to learn during the lesson (the lesson objectives)
- Generate interest in the topic (curiosity, relevance, links with other parts of the curriculum, use of stimulus material, etc.)
- Recap on previous learning through a question and answer session
- Find out what they know about the present topic (correct understanding and misconceptions)

Managing the pupils' learning

- Check that the pupils are on task
- Provide support and encouragement
- Praise good work
- Challenge pupils' thinking
- Check the time and shorten or lengthen the time allotted for the task if necessary
- If pupils are working in groups or individually try not to disrupt the flow of their work by making frequent announcements

Organizing the pupils for learning

- Explain what pupils are going to do
- Explain any science that pupils need to know at this stage
- Ask questions to check that pupils understand
- Encourage pupils to ask you questions about the topic
- Provide pupils with the necessary resources
- Tell pupils how long they have to complete the activity and what you expect the outcome to be

Moving the class on

- Ensure that all the pupils completely stop one activity so that they can concentrate on listening to you
- Spend a few moments going through what the pupils have learnt from the first task
- Explain the next task and check for understanding

There may be a number of different activities for the pupils to do in the lesson but care must be taken not to make the lesson too fragmented

Ending the lesson

- Warn the pupils that the lesson will end in 5–10 minutes time
- Find out what the pupils have learnt
- Through class discussion draw together the key points from the lesson
- Pack away the resources used
- Set homework, if appropriate
- Praise pupils for academic work and behaviour, if appropriate
- Dismiss the class on time and in an orderly fashion

Figure 3.5 *A suggested sequence of events in a lesson*

their mentor and tutor happy. They feel that as long as they have a rough idea of where they are going in a lesson, they can rely on textbooks and other resources supplied by the school and 'wing it'. This is likely to result in a poorly focused lesson with pupils having little idea of what they should be doing and when they should be doing it. The learning may be confused and pupils may be left with a feeling of not having achieved anything by the end of the period.

Either while you are working through the plan or when you have finished you will find it worthwhile to spend a little time going through the different phases of the lesson and thinking about what you will be doing and what the pupils will be doing. Sometimes quite small things, such as getting equipment to pupils, can cause major problems if they haven't been thought through properly.

5 STARTING THE LESSON

In the first five to ten minutes of the lesson you need to establish the atmosphere and the mood for the rest of the lesson. A lesson that begins noisily or looks disorganized can be difficult to re-establish and quite often continues in the same vane. You need to convey certain messages to the pupils and these are best done by the way you conduct yourself and what you get the pupils to do. Figure 3.6 lists some suggestions for activities during the first few minutes of a lesson. You will find it helpful to have some sort of structured routine and will find it beneficial to observe how experienced teachers interact with pupils during the early stages of a lesson.

Pupils benefit from having some idea of where they are going in a lesson. It shouldn't be a haphazard journey, moving from one activity to another with pupils having little idea of what they are supposed to be learning. There are various ways of conveying this information to pupils and you will find it useful to experiment with different techniques until you find something that is suitable for each of the classes you have. Basically, what you have to do is convert the objectives you have identified for the lesson into a form that can be readily understood by the pupils. One method is to talk to the class about what they are going to achieve.

e.g. (i) 'What we are going to today is . . . And by the end of the lesson you should understand why it is important to . . .'
(ii) 'What I am looking for in this lesson is to see if you can explain . . .'
(iii) 'The reason we are doing this is because . . .'

Another approach is to write the objectives either on the board or on a piece of paper that can be stuck into pupils' books. In this way the pupils have the lesson targets in front of them throughout the lesson enabling you to refer back to them as the work proceeds. You can use it as a checklist to monitor pupils' understanding, consolidate learning and know when you can safely move on to the next part of the lesson.

Action	Reason
Line up the pupils outside the room or, when this is not possible or pacticable, stand by the door as they enter.	Gives you an early opportunity to demonstrate that you are in charge. Provides you with an opportunity to talk to individuals about behaviour (both good and bad) and quality of work (praise and censure). Simply saying hello to individuals by name and asking how they are helps to develop relationships.
Organize a task for the pupils to do as soon as they sit down.	Helps the pupils to settle down and gives the message that they are going to do some 'serious work' during the lesson.
Establish a routine for coats, books and bags and stick to it.	You need to keep down the time taken for the class to settle down. If you let them chat they will want to continue their conversations into the lesson.
Take the register.	It helps to establish quiet. Some teachers take it later on in the lesson, particularly if there are likely to be pupils who will arrive late.
Recap of the previous lesson's work.	It stresses the importance of building on previous knowledge and, in most cases, links into the new work.
Finding out what pupils already know about the new topic.	A brainstorming activity or a series of questions to the class helps to identify prior knowledge and spot any misconceptions held by pupils.
Tell the pupils what they are going to learn today (i.e. tell them the lesson objectives in a language that they can understand) and write it on the board.	This helps to focus pupils' attention on the learning outcomes and acts as a checklist at the end of the lesson.

Figure 3.6 *Suggestions for procedures and activities at the start of a lesson*

6 THE MIDDLE PART

Having introduced the topic in the early part of the lesson, and hopefully whetted their appetite, you now need to develop the theme through a series of activities. What you choose to do will depend to a large extent on your confidence and your knowledge of teaching techniques. You need to choose activities that will enable the pupils to meet the objectives you have set for the

Low-level tasks	High-level tasks
Listening to the teacher	Finding out information for themselves
Copying from the board	Writing about how the science learnt can apply in different situations
Repeating an experiment demonstrated by the teacher	Planning an experiment, carrying it out and evaluating how it went
Memorizing science 'facts'	Using the science to explain a variety of phenomena
Filling in the blanks on worksheets	Writing a few paragraphs that involves putting together ideas from a number of areas of science
Repeating work covered earlier in the course	Providing pupils with new challenges that may require them to check on their own understanding
Reading around the class	Providing pupils with tasks that require them to use their imagination

Figure 3.7 *Tasks requiring different levels of cognitive demand*

lesson. As you work through your planning of the lesson you may move backwards and forwards between activities and objectives, making adjustments until you come up with something that you judge to be appropriate.

If you find that much of the lesson is teacher dominated, i.e. you are spending a lot of time talking to the class, then you should think of ways of getting the pupils involved. Some students like the sound of their own voice so much they can spend half the lesson or more pouring out information to the pupils. Remember you are not giving a lecture to dedicated undergraduates but a lesson to young people, who prefer to have interesting things to do.

You will also need to consider the intellectual demand of the tasks (see Figure 3.7) and appreciate that at certain times of the day pupils are going to be more receptive to work requiring a high cognitive demand than at others.

7 THE END OF THE LESSON

All teachers find themselves in a situation where the end of the lesson creeps up on them unexpectedly but it is something you should try to avoid. If you find that you are shouting '*finish that off for homework*' as they disappear out of the door then you have badly misjudged the time and there is little chance that the pupils will do the homework. In a good lesson there would be time for consolidating the learning at the end through activities such as: whole class discussion; question and answer; or pupil presentations. The KS3 National Science Strategy refers to this part of the lessson as a plenary. This gives you the opportunity to refer back to the lesson objectives and get pupils to judge for themselves as to whether they have been achieved. You will find it helpful to glance at your watch occasionally to check if you are running out of time. If you are, you should be prepared to curtail what the pupils are doing and allow a suitable slot for rounding things off. Pupils tend to remember the 'take home message' you send them away with more than the other things that go on during the lesson.

8 WHAT'S WRONG WITH FOLLOWING THE TEXTBOOK?

A tremendous amount of time, effort and money goes into the production of science textbooks. Most of the new books come complete with teachers' guides, assessment packs, activity and homework packs and integrated software. These are excellent resources and they will be a great help to you in preparing your lessons but they are not a replacement for lesson preparation. In order to use these materials effectively you will need to take 'ownership' of the contents. In doing this you will consider the various parts of the lesson and make a judgement as to their value in achieving your objectives. You may also have to consider what sort of gloss or spin you are going to put on each of the activities and whether or not you want to replace one or more of them. If you don't take ownership of the material there is a distinct danger that even the very best resource will produce a flat and uninteresting lesson.

9 SCHEMES OF WORK

A scheme of work (SoW) is a long-term planning document for the teaching of each science topic. It is one of the key documents that you will need to consult in your teaching practice school when planning your lessons. It will give you an idea as to where any one lesson fits into the teaching of the whole topic. By looking at the sequence of lessons you will be able to see how the teachers have built in continuity of experiences for the pupils. A SoW for KS3 will be based around the NC and possibly around the KS3 textbook the science department has decided to adopt.

A SoW can be used for:

- monitoring the types of activities used in lessons;
- checking that the activities match the objectives;

- planning for coverage and continuity of the curriculum;
- providing information when someone has to cover for absent members of staff.

Some textbook packages have an associated teachers' guide that contains most, if not all, the information you would expect to find in a SoW. A KS4 SoW will be based on the GCSE specification and, as well as referring to the course content, it is likely to contain cross-referencing to past questions. The production pof a SoW by a member of the science department, while time consuming, is a valuable experience in terms of thinking through what pupils will learn over a period of time and looking at the range of activities they will be involved in. Clearly, SoWs will need to be updated regularly as lessons are evaluated and as the NC changes, so it is a good idea to produce the documents on a word processor. Different schools will have different views on the layout and content but you would usually find that they contain the following information:

- *Statements relating to the philosophy and aims of the science course* – these will probably link to the 'mission statement' for the school and will indicate what the school and department are trying to achieve with the pupils.

- *Objectives for individual lessons* – this helps to map out the continuity of learning.

- *Outline lesson plans* – this enables the range of activities experienced by the pupils to be monitored. It will indicate how the teacher can provide for differentiation.

- *Opportunities for teaching the common requirements of the NC, The Nature of Science and Communication in Science* – it is worthwhile identifying these NC issues separately to make sure they are taught. It would be easy to go through a topic and forget to include them.

- *Homework tasks* – homework needs to be planned into the teaching scheme to ensure that all pupils in a year group have the same, or similar, experiences.

- *Resources to be used* – this helps the teacher and the technician plan ahead and make sure that equipment is booked. It is helpful to include cross-referencing to where resources are kept and to give page number references to textbooks and other written materials.

- *Practical tasks* – this would provide you with an outline of the practical and an indication of what equipment would be required, perhaps cross-referenced to a technician's list. It should also give some idea about the approach that can be used with the practical, e.g. how the task can be presented to the pupils in order to develop their investigative skills. Any safety precautions should be identified at this stage with an indication as to where to get more information if necessary.

- *Opportunities for using ICT* – this gives the teacher advanced warning about booking resources, such as the Computer Room. It also helps to plot the ICT experiences of the pupils so that they can be matched against their ICT work in other subjects and core ICT lessons.

- *Note of any prior learning that is required to understand the topic and/or common misconceptions that pupils may have* – this highlights things that a teacher needs to look out for when considering the learning activities for a lesson.

- *New words and/or key phrases that are to be learnt during the lesson* – this list focuses the teacher's attention on key aspects of language that pupils need to familiarize themselves with and use in the lesson.

- *Opportunities for assessment* – this section would contain an outline of how learning could be monitored on a lesson by lesson basis and indicate anything special that you should look out for, e.g. opportunities for pupils to apply their knowledge to new situations, common errors, ways of providing useful feedback to pupils.

QCA have produced specimen SoWs for both KS2 and KS3 science (*www.standards.dfes.gov.uk/schemes/*) with the view that these would aid teachers in interpreting the NC and, by having schemes that go across the two phases of education, help with continuity. The KS3 National Science Strategy is closely linked to the SoW and promotes the enquiry-based and constructionist approaches emphasized in the scheme. They contain plenty of good ideas and guidance on progression and the development of language, and, as such, are an invaluable resource for any science department. It is very tempting for schools to adopt the SoW lock, stock and barrel, for in doing so they can rest assured that they will cover all aspects of the NC. They may also believe that they have covered the work in a way that is compatible with KS3 national tests. If teachers do go down this route then it could be argued that they have lost a considerable amount of their professionalism as not only is the content of the curriculum being dictated to them (through the NC document) but also they are being directed about the way in which the subject is taught (through the SoW).

Where do you start from? There are a number of possibilities and your choice would probably be determined by your level of expertise in the topic. You could start by writing a concept map looking at the links between the key issues or you may turn to published science map (see, for example, Driver *et al.*, 1994a). These will enable you to get a flow of ideas that can be fitted together into a teaching sequence. Another route is to look at a series of textbooks and examine the way in which the work is structured. Some series of books have accompanying teachers' guides that contain teaching outlines and brief lesson notes. Alternatively, you may wish to take an existing SoW such as the QCA document and modify it.

In reviewing a SoW you would need to look at the level of detail given, perhaps using the list above as a guide. You need to make a judgement about how prescriptive you think the document ought to be and then see what sort of answers you get to the following questions:

- What guidance is there on how concepts and skills are to be developed?
- How does it link to the broader school aims?
- How is continuity built into the scheme?
- How does it relate to the NC?
- Does it cater for pupils of different abilities?
- Does it suggest that a variety of teaching activities could be used?

- Does it suggest a variety of practical activities including investigations?
- Are the risk assessments clear?

Practical activity 3.5

Look at the SoW for a particular topic from different sources: your school science department; a KS3 teachers' guide; the QCA SoW.

How easy is it to access information from each of the layouts?

How user friendly is the document in terms of helping you to plan your lessons?

As a new entrant to the teaching profession are there things that you would like to see included in a SoW that are not present in the ones you are reviewing?

What are the pros and cons of being provided with a SoW, such as the one from QCA, over writing one yourself (see Henderson, 2000 and Monk, 2000)?

What are the pros and cons of have a very tightly defined SoW?

CONCLUSION

Planning lessons is quite a complex intellectual exercise requiring you to hold a considerable amount of information in your head at any one time. You can go on and on reading more textbooks to see how each one presents the topic and thinking about what particular individuals will do under certain circumstances. You may then get to a state where you become muddled and not sure what to do. The best thing to do in the early stages is to keep it as simple as possible. Take things step by step, look at one or two ways of teaching the lesson, make a decision as to which suits both you and the class best and go with it.

CHAPTER 4

Getting to grips with teaching

INTRODUCTION

There are a number of important skills that you will have to learn in order to become an effective teacher. Many of these don't come naturally and some will take a considerable length of time to perfect. For example, if a pupil says something that is inappropriate, the natural reaction might be to shout at him or her. However, this may be entirely the wrong way of approaching the situation and it may lead to a deterioration of the circumstances. This chapter together with your classroom experiences will help you to make the right sorts of decisions in managing pupils and controlling their behaviour. The chapter goes on to examine the key skill of communicating with pupils through explanations and oral questioning. You will find it helpful to observe experienced teachers carrying out these skills and to monitor your own progress.

By the end of this chapter you should:

- understand a number of the key facets of classroom management;
- understand the important principles of classroom control;
- know how to structure the explanation of science concepts;
- know how to ask questions and deal with pupils' responses.

1   CLASSROOM MANAGEMENT

Classroom management is about managing and organizing situations and people to ensure that learning can take place. In this chapter we will take a look at some of the overarching principles of management which are taken up in other chapters in relation to specific teaching techniques.

Time is probably one of the most difficult things we all have to manage during our daily lives, there just isn't enough of it, and yet in the classroom you have to be a past master at time management. The starting point is knowing the time of the lessons and any idiosyncrasies of the bell, together with having a watch set to school time. The next step is knowing when to switch from one activity to another. This is best done by keeping an eye on different groups of pupils, checking their progress and using your professional judgement. You then have to think about how you are going to bring one phase of the lesson to a close and how you are going to take them through to the next part. In most cases this will involve stopping all the class, making sure they are listening to you and talking to them about what they have just done, followed by an explanation of what they are about to do. Sounds easy doesn't it, but you may come across one or two little problems, such as not all pupils finishing the first task at the same time and loss of impetus. In these cases you need to decide about when, or if, the slower workers should complete their work and how you are going to generate enthusiasm for the next task. You need to make sure that all pupils are paying attention to you during this transition and not allow pupils to try to finish off work or to chat. Sometimes pupils see this break as an opportunity for a well-deserved rest and a time for a quick catch up with the latest gossip.

The end of the lesson shouldn't come as a surprise to you. You need to manage the timing of the lesson so that you can comfortably draw things to a conclusion, pack the materials away and dismiss the pupils in an orderly fashion.

In addition to managing time you will need to manage what pupils do in the time available to them. In your planning it is important that you think about differentiation (see p. 160) and matching tasks to pupils' ability. During the lesson you will have to consider how to manage pupils' engagement with the tasks. For example, as the lesson progresses you may need to make decisions about changing:

- the level of difficulty of the work (modifying tasks or providing additional information);
- the 'size' of the piece of work (breaking the information down into suitably sized, manageable chunks);
- the momentum in order to maintain or promote motivation.

If you see that a group of pupils are not working as hard as you would like them to do there are a number of strategies you could employ. You could turn to them and tell them to stop talking and get on with their work. You could go up to them and ask them how they are getting on (e.g. 'Let's have a look at what you have written so far.' 'Have you remembered to include . . .?'). You could provide them with some additional information (e.g. 'Right now there are one or two other things that are interesting about this.' 'What you need to be thinking about is . . .') followed by a few pertinent questions.

Another aspect of management is the movement of pupils, getting them seated at the start of the lesson, moving them for different types of activities (e.g. to obtain equipment for a practical, coming round the front for a demonstration, sitting them around a TV and video) and dismissing them at the end of the lesson. It is easy to dismiss this believing it to be trivial, thinking that pupils can organize their own movement, but you will find that there are a number of benefits associated with it. It helps to reinforce the fact that you are in charge and bring a sense of order and discipline to the lesson. It can also reduce the number of silly classroom squabbles of who sits where.

Practical activity 4.1

Consider a number of different strategies that could be used for keeping pupils on task during a lesson. What are the advantages and disadvantages of each of the methods you have selected?

How can you make judgements about the effectiveness of a learning activity during a lesson?

2 | MANAGING BEHAVIOUR

Discipline is probably the main concern of all student teachers as they enter an ITE course and yet, in reality, most pupils are very pleasant individuals who are quite keen to get on with the work and are not interested in disrupting the class. Some teachers invite indiscipline by the way they act in the classroom. This is typified by teachers who 'can't be bothered' and let pupils get away with things which over a very short period of time results in very negative attitudes from the pupils towards both the teacher and the subject. Discipline problems can be significantly reduced if pupils can see that you care about what they are learning and are interested in them as individuals. One of the first things that you should give priority to is learning pupils' names and using them as much as you can. You will be surprised when you see how effective one or two simple routines are in controlling a class. The best disciplinarians are not those who rant and rave at pupils. Good disciplinarians are often quiet and calm and are consistent and fair in their use of punishment. You will need to establish yourself as a person who can keep good class control very early on in your teaching experience and will then have to maintain a good level of discipline. You need to be aware of the 'honeymoon period' when you start teaching any class. The pupils may be well behaved for a week or two while they work out what sort of a person you are and what they can get away with. As soon as you relax, thinking that the class poses no problems, the pupils seize the opportunity and start to eat away at your control. You will find it helpful to use the following tried and tested techniques.

2.1 Routines

You need to establish a number of different routines so that pupils feel comfortable in an environment where they know what to expect and what is expected of them. At the start of a lesson you might line pupils up in the corridor outside the laboratory and have a few words with them outside or you may stand in the doorway and say something to individuals as they enter. This meeting and greeting routine helps to develop a relationship with them. It is an opportunity to give a friendly welcome or praise or have a word about behaviour. You need to have a routine for coats, books and bags whereby pupils get out what is necessary for the lesson and put other things out of the way. Pupils don't always bring pens and books with them so it is a good idea to have a set system where they can borrow equipment for the lesson. Reduce the number of opportunities for pupils to make a fuss over trivial things.

2.2 Non-verbal interactions

You must look as though you are in control. You can do this by adopting a confident posture (standing upright, looking alert), giving the pupils the message that this is your territory and that here they must abide by your rules. Keep your arms by your side. Folding them could look too aggressive and putting them in your pockets might look too relaxed. It is a good idea not to fiddle with things and to keep your hands free in order that you can use them for giving additional emphasis to what you are saying. Always address the pupils from a position where they can all see you and you can see them. Eye contact alone can stop some discipline problems and you will find it useful to scan the class frequently to check how they are reacting to what is going on in the lesson. You could supplement this with some facial gestures indicating pleasure or annoyance with pupils, together with some appropriate gestures. If you point at somebody it is a good idea to say the name of the person to make it exactly clear who you are referring to. You should move around the room when pupils are working so that the pupils get the message that you are never too far away.

2.3 Use of praise

Some teachers are very good at telling pupils off for poor behaviour but they forget about giving praise for good behaviour. Telling pupils that they have worked well can have enormous benefits for their self-esteem and their attitude towards their work. You have got to choose the right sort of language so that it sounds sincere and you have got to be careful not to overdo it otherwise you end up devaluing it. There will be occasions where you will praise pupils in front of the whole class, for example when answering an oral question correctly. There will be other times when you think that it is better to praise pupils individually to avoid embarrassment.

2.4 Rules and punishments

Your rules, which need to be consistent with the school rules, need to be made explicit to the pupils. The first time you see a pupil breaking a rule, e.g. talking out of turn, you need to do something about it. It is no use saying to yourself, 'I'll ignore it this time and I'm sure he won't do it again' because the chances are that he will see that he got away with it the first time round and will try again. For a minor misdemeanour it is probably sufficient to signal to the pupil, through facial expression, gesture and a few well-chosen words, that you have registered that something has been done and that you don't want it to happen again. Whenever possible you should try not to disrupt the flow of the lesson. Disruption could be what the pupil is aiming for and by minimizing it you have shown that the pupil cannot get his/her own way. You should have at the back of your mind an idea about what punishment fits what crime. These have got to be reasonable and fair. If there is confusion as to who has done what you should try to get to the bottom of it, but not during lesson time. Some schools have adopted an assertive discipline system (Canter and Canter, 1993) linked to a graded list of consequences. Pupils know the ground rules for every lesson and what will happen if they break them. The system starts with a clear warning signal being given by writing the pupil's name on the board, which in most cases is enough to deter pupils from further misbehaviour.

2.5 Use of your voice

If you constantly have to raise your voice to be heard, then there is something wrong. You shouldn't talk over pupils. You may need raise your voice to get attention with something like 'Stop, what you are doing and listen to me' and then you can give the instruction in a clear, calm manner. You need to be polite and in control. It is unwise to be sarcastic as some pupils react very badly to this sort of treatment. Sometimes you may find it more effective to have a quiet word with a pupil about behaviour rather than admonish him/her in public.

2.6   Moving pupils

Moving pupils to somewhere where their behaviour can be monitored more closely, such as the table next to you, can work to good effect as young people don't like being separated from their friends. However, you need to be aware that the movement alone may not stop the disruption, in fact it may exacerbate the situation for a pupil who was previously talking to his neighbour now may feel the need to turn round and shout to this person. You also need to look out for those pupils that you move and who mysteriously slide back into their original position.

Practical activity 4.2

Make sure that you are familiar with the discipline policy within your school before you start teaching. What support mechanisms are in place in the school? How does the school encourage pupils to be well behaved in addition to punishing them for poor behaviour? While it is not always possible to analyse breaches of discipline you will find it valuable to ask yourself why pupils react in a particular way. Was there something you could have done to have avoided the problem?

Ask to observe a class that contains some particularly disruptive pupils being taught by a teacher who has a good reputation for dealing with such children. Try to analyse how the teacher manages to control them.

3   PREPARING YOURSELF

Pupils are very good at picking up weaknesses in teachers. They can tell if you are nervous or not fully in control of the situation from the sound of your voice and from your body language. You can make significant improvements to your classroom control by using a few simple techniques, such as:

- Work out in advance what you are going to do if pupils misbehave.
- Put yourself in the right frame of mind before the lesson starts by telling yourself that you are the person in control. Carry out a few deep breathing exercises to calm yourself down. This is particularly useful if you have had a bad experience with the class the lesson before. At the start of the lesson, slow everything down. Control your nerves by deep breathing and talking slowly.
- You may be tense because of the memory of pupils' previous misbehavior and

be worried about what is going to happen this time. One way of helping you to keep calm is to remind yourself that nothing lasts forever. You can take the edge off the nervousness by thinking about something pleasant that you are going to do in the not too distant future.

- You can convey all sorts of message by the way you look. Ask yourself if a change of hairstyle would have any affect on your authority in the classroom. Relaxed clothing can sometimes give the impression that discipline is relaxed. Power dressing can help to give the impression that you are in control. However, you have got to be careful that you don't go over the top as this could have a very negative effect. You should dress in a manner that is similar to the upper end of the dress code used by teachers in the school.

The following extract from an Ofsted report on attendance and discipline highlights some key examples of good practice.

> Here teachers established the full attention of the whole class before they began the lesson; there were clear and well understood conventions about, for example, the manner in which pupils entered the room and how they prepared and waited. The teachers often paid particular attention to the more reluctant, making it clear that their compliance was needed before the lesson could start. The lessons opened with a clear statement of what the pupils were to do during the lesson and what they were to achieve by its end. There was a variety of activities and timing was good, with the teacher intervening and refocusing attention to prevent distraction; the approach showed the benefits of training pupils to co-operate with one another so as to use the lesson time productively. During the lesson, whenever necessary but without breaking the flow, pupils were reminded of the need to listen attentively, to take turns in answering, and to be otherwise considerate.
>
> (Ofsted, 2001)

4   COMMUNICATING WITH PUPILS

You will have your own views about what constitutes 'good teaching', possibly based around a teacher that you looked up to in school and who inspired you to go on to study science at university. Initially you may try to emulate them but you will soon realise that your personality and way of working is different. Some students start off by thinking that the most important thing about teaching is to 'cover' as much content as possible in one lesson. They would tend to favour a transmission style of teaching using a lot of chalk and talk, presenting information in a very didactic manner. This type of approach is not likely to result in any deep learning. Pupils may be able to give you back what you have given them but would find it difficult to go beyond that.

The first step in pupils' learning often involves the teacher giving information to the pupils together with some directions as to how to use the information. In doing this you need to think about the composition of the class and their ability to understand the concepts being taught. In delivering your explanation you will need to keep a close eye on pupils' reactions by watching their body language and listening to the comments and questions they pose.

5 EXPLANATIONS AND GIVING INSTRUCTIONS

Everybody thinks that teaching is easy if you know your 'stuff', but once you have tried explaining something to a group of pupils only to find that the majority of them didn't understand you soon change your opinion. A good explanation is clear and well structured. It shouldn't be too long as pupils may loose the thread of the argument. Some inexperienced teachers think that when pupils are sitting quietly listening to you, they are taking every word in and thoroughly understanding it. Explanations can come at various points in the lesson but are generally at the beginning to clarify or teach concepts required during the lesson or at the end as part of the drawing together of key ideas. You would find it helpful to consider the following steps when planning and delivering explanations.

Planning
Write down the key ideas that pupils need to grasp in order to understand your explanation. Sometimes explanations fail because a teacher misses out a key point, either because they believed it to be obvious or because they simply forgot to mention it.

The lead in
Try to generate an interest in what you are about to say. This could be done by linking the new material to previous work or stressing that what you are explaining is important for the understanding of work to be done. It could arise out of pupils' answers to your questions or from pupils asking their own questions. Sometimes you will be able to generate interest by telling a short story that leads in to the science. Although this may seem contrived, pupils tend to enjoy it and go along with your yarn even to the point that it helps them to remember things.

What it is we are trying to explain
Pupils may have some preconceived ideas of what it is you are trying to explain. They will have mental images that may be quite remote from the truth. Abstract concepts may be seen in very concrete terms or pupils may be confused with similar sounding words. You need to be very clear in defining what type of thing you are explaining and clarify any science terminology you are going to use.

Provide examples, analogies and models
Quite often the penny drops when pupils relate the explanation to something that they are familiar with. Working through a number of examples with the class will help pupils to see patterns and be able to formulate generalized statements. However, if you use examples that don't quite fit the rule or involve complex scenarios then you will cause confusion. Only when you are satisfied that pupils have understood the general rule should you go on to look at slightly different examples.

Models are particularly useful in explaining things that pupils cannot see, such as the movement of particles, the flow of electricity and the movement of the planets. You need to make the pupils aware of what exactly the model represents. The types of models that you might use would fall into one of the following categories:

- scale models (a version of the original that is easy to see, e.g. anatomical models);

- analogue models (a simplification of the original used to explain certain phenomena (e.g. different types of atomic and molecular models);

- mathematical models (expressing a situation in terms of formulae, e.g. gas laws, further examples are given in Figure 6.4);

- theoretical models (these put forward an explanation of a situation based on previous scientific knowledge, experiences and observations (e.g. the big bang theory).

It is a good idea to get pupils to use models and to appreciate what type of model they are. This can be linked in to discussions about the nature of science and how scientists use this approach to help them to explain the results of their experiments. Some useful examples of modelling activities can be found in *The Nature of Science* (Warren, 2001a).

Using diagrams
Some pupils have difficulty visualizing what teachers say and a picture or diagram on the board helps to make things clearer. You could use a piece of chart paper or a large diagram together with words or symbols that you stick onto it with 'Velcro' or 'Blu-tack'. For example when teaching about ion formation you could have diagrams of sodium and chlorine atoms containing stuck on electrons. This enables electron transfer and the charge on the ion to be easily shown. You may think that this sounds rather 'naff' but you will find that by playing on the childish nature of the model pupils will remember it.

Using small tasks
Small practical tasks followed by questions can illustrate the point you are trying to get across.

Emphasizing key words
Key words or new words will need to be explained and written on the board for emphasis.

Using key phrases
There are certain phrases you can use to alert pupils to the significance of what you are saying. Here are a few of them:

- 'Now, this is an important point . . .'

- 'I want you to pay particular attention to this . . .'

- 'The first point I want to make is . . .'

Pace of delivery

You need to bear in mind that when you speak to a class rather than an individual you must speak more slowly to make sure that everyone 'captures' your words. Also, without labouring the point, you should repeat important sentences. You could try using phrases such as:

- 'Ok, now lets just say that again . . .'
- 'Mary, can you tell me again what I just said . . .?' 'Andrew what do you understand by . . .?'
- 'Right, let's write that down before we go on.'

Going through things a step at a time

If there is a sequence that needs to be followed in the explanation it is worth considering numbering the points, such as:

- 'First we need to look at . . .'
- 'Secondly, there are . . .'
- 'Thirdly, we need to take into account . . .'
- 'And finally . . .'

Maintaining the flow

A clear explanation will not contain too many 'ums' and 'ers'. Some teachers also get carried away and go off at a tangent, bringing in all sorts of irrelevant information that will lead to confusion. It is important to realize that what you are explaining is likely to be difficult for most pupils and they need to keep focused on the main points. You will find that, even having given a brilliant explanation and received correct answers to your questions, there will still be pupils who have not understood. For example, in a recent lesson I observed, the student teacher had given an excellent explanation of expansion on heating. She then went on to demonstrate the bending of a bi-metallic strip and asked the pupils to tell her what they thought was happening. There were a mixture of ideas and eventually they came up with the correct solution which she emphasized. The pupils were then asked to write about it in their own words. Many of the pupils wrote correct explanations but some didn't. This is what Laura wrote:

> When you have this strip the heavier metal (steel) will push the lighter metal (brass) down, because the particles from the steel have gone further apart down the strip causing the bi-metallic strip to fall downwards.

Laura had mixed up some of the ideas from the teacher with some of the incorrect responses from other pupils who thought that the bending had something to do with gravity. You will only pick up misunderstandings like this by asking pupils to put things into their own words.

6 | CONSIDERING VOCABULARY

Pupils can become confused simply because they don't understand the meaning of some of the words used in science lessons. They get words mixed up for a variety of reasons, for example:

- words that sound similar (e.g. isotope and allotrope);
- words that begin or end with the same group of letters (e.g. poly-, -graph);
- words that have different meanings in science and in everyday use (e.g. solution, work, power);
- words that are often used in a scientifically incorrect way in everyday use e.g. weight – meaning mass, heat – referring to temperature, melt – meaning dissolve).

Pupils will also get other scientific words mixed up because they don't understand the differences or have misconceptions about the ideas involved, e.g. galaxy and universe, the greenhouse effect and the hole in the ozone layer, atom and molecule.

Another group of words that pupils have difficulty with consists of some everyday words that we, as adults, are completely familiar with but some pupils have not fully grasped the meaning as yet. These include common words such as:

constant	effect	source	system	excess	complex
device	preparation	surround	abundant	negligible	accumulate

Clearly if pupils do not understand words you are using in your explanations then they are not going to understand the scientific concepts being taught. You will need to keep a close check on the language you use and look for signs of misunderstanding among your pupils. There are a number of things that you can do to help, such as:

- building up a poster display of new science words as they occur in the teaching;
- insisting that pupils construct a dictionary of difficult words at the back of their exercise books;
- asking pupils to construct sentences that include the new words;
- using games or quizzes that link words with their meaning;
- asking the pupils to produce concept maps.

7 | QUESTIONING

Asking questions to a group of pupils is not as easy as it might first appear. Inexperienced teachers fire questions at the class and receive a tirade of answers, frequently indecipherable and from unidentifiable pupils. The questions tend to be at the start of the lesson and are mainly concerned with what happened last time the pupils had science. While it is a good idea to recap what went on during the last lesson it is important to use a strategy that is not going to lead to overexcitement and shouting out and one that is going to involve more than memory jogging. If you think about why teachers ask questions you will soon realize that there are many reasons other than checking that pupils have remembered previously taught work. Kerry (1998) identifies the following reasons for asking questions:

- to provide pupils with the opportunity to talk constructively on task;
- to provide pupils with the opportunity to express their views;
- to encourage a problem-solving approach to thinking;
- to help pupils externalize and verbalize knowledge;
- to encourage thinking aloud;
- to help pupils learn from, and respect, one another;
- to monitor the extent of and deficiencies in pupils' learning;
- to deepen thinking levels and improve conceptualization.

There are two broad categories of questions: open questions where there are a variety of acceptable responses and closed questions where there is usually one correct response. Examples are:

Open questions	Closed questions
'What do you think would happen if . . .?'	'What was the colour of the indicator . . .?'
'What sorts of things would make a good . . .?'	'What is the special name we give to the . . .?'
'Who can tell me what we did last lesson?'	'How many main body parts do insects have?'
'How did we find out about . . .?'	'Which three things did we change in the investigation?'

8 | QUESTIONING TECHNIQUE

Questioning then is not simply a procedure for finding out what pupils have remembered. A question and answer session can be a useful learning experience for all the pupils if it is handled correctly. The first stage is setting the right climate for the session, and that means ensuring that you don't have to endure a lot of shouting out of answers. If pupils shout out you may be unsure as to who has answered, making it less easy to continue with the follow on question, and it can create a noisy environment where it is difficult for anyone to think. You could ask the pupils to put their hands up, but a better way is to ask them by name. This gives you the opportunity to target specific questions to individuals. You may want to do this for a variety of reasons, such as matching the level of a question to the ability of a pupil, checking on the progress made by certain individuals, or getting the attention of pupils who are not concentrating. You need to think about the distribution of questions around the group, trying to involve equal numbers of boys and girls and making sure that you don't forget those pupils who are not in your immediate arc of vision. It is worth considering moving around the class and stopping to ask questions. This way you keep the pupils on their toes and can keep an eye on pupils' reactions. It is important to ensure that the session does not become a discussion between the teacher and one or two pupils. Clearly you will not have time to ask everyone a question, but by creating a situation where nobody knows who will be asked next you can keep all members of the class mentally involved.

9   SOME IDEAS FOR ASKING QUESTIONS

- Don't forget praise (for the correct answers and for trying).
- Provide the pupils with some input (e.g. reminder of general issues from last lesson, or a description of a scenario from everyday life on which the topic of the day is going to be based).
- Ask several relatively simple recall questions (warm-up procedure, helping to promote confidence).
- Ask questions that test understanding (e.g. 'Chris, why did you think that happened?' 'Paul, which of those was the best?' 'Jackie, can you explain to everyone why it did that?').
- Open the questions up to others (e.g. 'Ok, Damien do you think Andrew is right?' 'Why?' 'Mark, what other evidence have we got for . . .?' 'Gail, if we had . . . instead of . . . what do you think would happen then?' 'Listen to someone else's answer. I'll come back to you in two minutes and I'll expect you to know the answer').
- During the part of the session when you are asking pupils to think and reflect on situations, you must allow time for pupils to answer.
- Ask questions that invite pupils to predict what would happen in different situations based on their previous knowledge (e.g. 'Donna, what do you think would happen if we used . . . instead of . . .?' 'Why?' 'Debbie, can you tell us what you would expect if we doubled the mass?' 'Why?' 'Matthew, how could you tell if something was happening?').
- Ask pupils to write down the answer to certain questions (e.g. 'Ok, for this one I would like you all to write down the answer on the paper I have given you.' 'Now Gail, will you please read out what you have written. Ok, thanks, now Sarah: what have you got?'). After collecting a few answers look at common responses and differences.

- Ask pupils questions that will lead to a summing up of the main points learnt during the lesson. (e.g. 'Aparna, can you remind us what we found out from the practical?' 'Josie, tell us again about . . .')

- Vary the pace of delivery. Use rapid fire questions from time to time and questions interspersed with pause for thought. Use gestures to emphasize important points, etc.

Even by involving a number of pupils in the ways described above you cannot be sure about what the rest of the class know. Selley (2000) has come up with some ideas that involve the whole class in answering questions:

1. *Small-group discussion*
   Divide the class up into groups of two to six pupils and give each group a card containing a series of questions. Allow a fixed time for the group to produce written answers on which all (or the majority) of members have agreed. The questions should not be ones requiring simple recall of information or, in this instance, questions involving a controversial science issue. The questions should be the type that requires pupils to think and apply their knowledge to different situations. The product from the activity could simply be the written responses or there could be a plenary discussion.

2. *Class decisions*
   Pupils as individuals or as representatives of groups put forward their answer to a question but instead of saying 'right' or 'wrong' the teacher asks others if they agree or disagree. Others may challenge the first group to ask for further explanation or they may put forward their alternative response.

Another method of involving more pupils is to supply each member of the class with three different coloured pieces of card, say red, green and orange. The cards can be given specific meanings dependant on the type of questions asked (see Figure 4.1). When a question is asked pupils are asked to hold up a card corresponding to their perception of the correct answer. The teacher looks at their responses and then follows this with supplementary questions to particular individuals. Further ideas about questioning and classifying questions can be found in papers by Car (1998) and Koufetta-Menicou and Scaife (2000).

Type of question	Red card	Green card	Orange card
Questions involving a yes or no reply	No	Yes	Not sure
Pupils are read a statement and they have to decide if it is true or false or sometimes true and sometimes false	False	True	Maybe true or maybe false
Multiple choice	A	B	C

Figure 4.1 *Using coloured cards to answer oral questions*

Practical activity 4.3

Use the list below to identify the use of questioning skills during lessons or parts of lessons observed. Make notes where appropriate, these will assist you in any follow-up discussion.

1. Key questions
- Make a note of the key questions and of supplementary questions.
- Note how the questions lead and develop the pupils' thinking.

2. Distribution of questions
- Make a plan of the class. Show the position of the teacher and any other key features. You may also wish to identify boys and girls and look at the distribution of questions to each group.
- For a specified period of time tick each pupil's name or position as the class is questioned.
- After the lesson discuss the distribution of questions and consider how effectively the whole class was involved.

3. Eye contact
- Note how the teacher makes effective eye contact. Is s/he still aware of the rest of the class?

4. Timing
- How long does the teacher wait for an answer?
- Are pupils given the time to develop an answer?

5. Prompting
- Are pupils who say they don't know encouraged to try again (possibly later)? Does the teacher rephrase or simplify the question, or go back a few steps, or give clues?
- How are unresponsive pupils encouraged?

6. Reinforcement
- Does the teacher praise or reward good answers and build up on half answers?
- How effectively does she/he deal with 'wrong' answers?

7. Language and vocabulary
- Note the level and clarity of the use of language.

8. Non-verbal clues
- Watch for and note how the teacher uses non-verbal behaviour to back up his/her use of questions.

(Adapted from Parkinson and Rowe, 1997, p. 381)

CHAPTER 5

Learning through writing and group discussion

In this chapter, and the following two chapters, you will have the opportunity to read about a number of teaching and learning activities used in science. In all of the activities described pupils are required to 'do things': writing, talking, working on a computer, carrying out practical work. The emphasis is on pupils being involved in the science and being active learners rather than passive participants in the lesson.

By the end of this chapter you should:

- know how to set a variety of science writing tasks and understand how this work will help pupils to learn;
- know how to organize group activities and understand how group discussion helps pupils to learn;
- understand how to use burr diagrams, concept maps and concept cartoons;
- know how to set up role play and drama activities and appreciate their contribution to pupils' learning;
- understand how the activities described in this chapter can be used to teach scientific enquiry;
- appreciate the importance of active learning.

1 PUPILS' WRITING

Some pupils see writing as a chore and something to be avoided at all costs in science lessons. They will say that they much prefer practical work. This message is sometimes reinforced by teachers who say things like 'hurry up and get through the writing and then we can get on with the experiment' and 'if you don't behave, we will stop doing the experiment and do some writing'. There are, of course, those pupils who actually enjoy writing and may prefer it to doing practical work. The way in which any task is introduced to a class will have a bearing on how they react to it. Experienced teachers are good at 'selling' tasks to their classes.

Right, today I've got something very interesting for you. What we're going to is put together a few ideas about what we've learnt in the last few lessons about particles as though we were sending an email to a friend who hadn't done this topic yet.

This sounds better than:

Today we are going to write a summary of what we have learnt about particles over the last few lessons.

Pupils can learn a great deal of science through writing activities, and by varying the type of activity it is possible to motivate pupils and bring in an element of fun from time to time (see Figure 5.1). Part of the job of science teachers is to raise pupils' levels of literacy and help them to use language to clarify their understanding of science concepts. If pupils' writing in science is restricted to filling in the blanks on worksheets and writing the odd sentence or two then they are unlikely to make a great deal of progress in their use of scientific vocabulary and their understanding of concepts will be limited. In designing writing tasks for pupils there are a number of things that need to be considered, such as:

- the age and ability of the pupils (e.g. ensuring that the needs of pupils who have difficulties with writing or spelling are catered for);
- the number of new technical words for the activity required (too many new words will make the task difficult);
- the amount of structuring and guidance given to the pupils (some tasks may require the teacher to produce writing frames to help pupils compose their work but this support should be removed as they progress);
- the types of activities that pupils are asked to do in other subjects (teachers of all subjects will be trying to raise pupils' literacy levels and there is a danger that pupils will be asked to do the same sort of thing over and over again. It is important to liaise with other subject teachers to find out what they are doing. In particular you should watch out for pupils being asked to do posters and newspaper articles in many of their subjects. While it is a good idea to use these approaches, pupils tend to get fed up if they are overdosed on the same type of activity in a lot of their lessons);
- the length of time it takes pupils to do the task;
- the amount of copying compared with how much of the task is the pupils' own writing (the work should be structured so that pupils do not copy work straight from books, CD-ROMs or the Internet);
- the extent to which the use of ICT can be used to advantage (e.g. drafting and redrafting work, moving scrambled text, spell-checking, collaborative writing opportunities – see p. 108);
- the amount of marking that it creates for the teacher (in order to help the pupils to make progress with their understanding of science and improve their literacy the work will need to be marked thoroughly).

2 | IDEAS FOR WRITING EXERCISES

It is possible to distinguish two types of writing normally carried out in science lessons: writing notes that can be used for revision purposes and writing exercises where the sole purpose is to give pupils the opportunity to learn about science. When the writing is required for revision, the teacher generally provides considerable structure and guidance reducing the possibility of pupils making mistakes. In a writing-for-learning exercise the pupil is given much more freedom, but may still require help in the construction of the piece of work. One way of doing this is to provide pupils with a writing frame which prompts them to say certain things at different stages of the work, and provides them with guidance on the writing style, e.g. tense of verbs, sense of audience, personal or formal. Writing frames are most commonly used, at present, to help pupils structure their writing up of science investigations to ensure that pupils include all the relevant information in the correct sequence.

You will need to make judgements about when to use writing frames and what level of detail you provide pupils with. In any one class you may choose to use writing frames that differ in structure to cater for individual pupil's needs. As time goes on you would probably reduce the support you provide to encourage pupils to think for themselves.

Practical activity 5.1

1. Consider how you would carry out a lesson where pupils are asked to write up a practical task. This would involve using the correct verb tense and they would need to be reminded that the instructions are given in the present tense but that they should write in the past tense.

2. Plan a series of writing frames for different scenarios, e.g. an explanation of a science concept, a piece of persuasive writing (e.g. healthy lifestyle), or discussing situations where there is more than one point of view.

In many cases the learning experience can be enhanced by allowing pupils to complete these exercises in groups, as this provides them with the opportunity to talk about the science involved. Further examples of writing exercises, linked to the use of ICT are given on page 109.

3 | POSTERS

Pupils can be asked to produce posters in a variety of settings, as shown in Figure 5.2. The production of posters helps to focus pupils' attention on the key points and, as such they can be used to draw things together at various stages during the teaching of a topic. While the number of words on the poster may be fairly limited, the thought processes that have gone into the production are

Idea	Comment
Labelling	Pupils use the information from the text to label a diagram or use information from a diagram to complete a text.
Converting a flow chart or diagram into words	Gives pupils the opportunity to interpret the meaning of the chart. The process can be done in reverse.
Rearranging text into the correct sequence	Jumbled text is given to pupils on a worksheet and the pupils have to rearrange it into the correct order. This could be done on the computer by placing the text in a text box and asking pupils to drag and drop.
A cloze procedure exercise	The trick in preparing these exercises is to make sure that the task matches the abilities of the target pupils. If the teacher provides the missing words the task is made easier. The task can be made harder by missing out words at regular intervals (e.g. every seventh word) or by missing out random words. Consider variations such as telling pupils that you have spilt liquid paper on the text or that the printer isn't working properly. This could give the pupils text with parts of words missing.
Writing a cartoon sketch	Pupils could be given a series of clipart characters and speech bubbles (produced on a word processor) and be asked to fill in the bubbles to make a cartoon strip.
Preparing a newspaper article	This could be a stick-and-paste exercise using pictures and pupils' handwritten text or it could be produced on the computer. Pupils can produce a professional looking piece of work, perhaps using pictures taken with a digital camera.
Using a word bank	Pupils are given the task of making sentences using words from the word bank derived from the topic being taught. Perhaps a prize for the pupil with the most sentences.
Preparing a poster	As above, this can be hand- or computer-produced. A good mix of large text and pictures is ideal for a poster. Posters placed around the room can provide useful reminders of work done.
Writing a letter	The teacher can choose different types of people (friend, adult with no science background, scientist, etc.) to be the recipients of the letter, dependent on the type of language skills she/he want the pupils to develop.
Writing from the position of being a fantasy figure	The pupil can write from the position of being a water droplet, a carbon atom or any other character that enables the pupil to write using the scientific concepts she/he has learnt.

Continued

Idea	Comment
Put into words what the graph tells you	Pupils interpret the shape of the graph and describe key features. Alternatively they can sketch a graph from a description (see similar exercises in Goldsworthy *et al.*, 1999, pp. 12 & 72).
Writing a technical report	In order to help pupils prepare for the more formal writing required in writing up their investigative work for GCSE they will need practise in this mode of writing.
Writing about a contoversy in science	Pupils can write about why certain scientific theories have not stood up to the test of time (for an example of background information see Talbot, 2000).
Asking pupils to write down a summary of what they have learnt during the topic	Rather than provide summaries for the pupils, consider asking pupils to search through what they have done and produce their own.
Asking pupils to write down a scientific explanation of an everyday event	Can be used at the beginning of a topic to identify pupils' prior understanding or at the end of a topic to check on pupils' learning.

Figure 5.1 *Ideas for writing exercises*

usually considerable. You need to try to avoid wasting time on trivial activities such as cutting out and pasting pictures on posters, e.g. pictures of domestic electrical appliances from magazines to illustrate the conversion of electrical energy into heat, light and sound, and get the pupils to think how they might depict situations through simple drawings and diagrams.

In order to help pupils improve the quality of their posters you could ask them to devise some criteria for judging them, such as: the number and type of illustrations, simplicity and clarity of explanations, how easy it is to read.

The ambiance of a laboratory can be improved considerably by the use of well-presented posters. These will probably be a mixture of those produced by

Practial activity 5.2

Look at the laboratories you work in and ask yourself what sort of image do these rooms give to pupils about science. Have a look at the wall displays in other subject areas and compare these to those found in the science rooms.

How often do you think wall displays should be changed?

Who do you think should be responsible for the displays?

Consider volunteering to help with room displays.

Type of poster	Features
Safety	Large colourful, eye catching, clear message. Placed in science laboratories.
Promoting healthy living	Format as above. Placed in laboratories and/or local health centres and community centres.
Summary of group discussion	Clear and easy to read. Placed in science laboratories on a temporary basis.
Topic	Key points (or learning objectives) are added each lesson. Placed in the laboratory.
Revision	Pupils construct individual revision posters that are kept in their books or at home.

Figure 5.2 *Examples of different types of posters*

the pupils; those produced by the teacher and some commercially produced posters. Figure 5.3 illustrates the sort of bright and cheerful images that can be displayed.

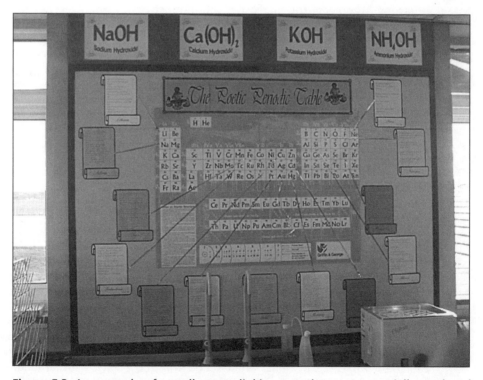

Figure 5.3 *An example of a wall poster linking together a commercially produced periodic table with samples of pupils' work*

4 | READING AND WRITING TASKS

In September 1998 the National Literacy Strategy was introduced into primary schools with the remit of helping pupils to read and write with confidence, fluency and understanding. Since then pupils entering the secondary school have been equipped with some key skills that can be used effectively by science teachers (McKeon, 2000). Pupils will have had experience of:

- locating information using indices, etc.;
- identifying different sorts of styles of writing including reporting and explaining;
- identifying key information (note-taking);
- creating summaries, skimming and scanning.

Over the last ten to fifteen years the amount of writing in year 11–16 science textbooks has considerably decreased to an extent where the visual effect of the page appears to have greater importance than the treatment of the science topic. It could be said that the amount of reading we require of pupils in science is very limited even though we know that pupils can learn a great deal by working their way through a piece of text. One of the reasons for moving away from text-laden material was to ensure that pupils' inability to comprehend written information did not get in the way of them learning science. There are a number of strong arguments for increasing the number of reading exercises in science lessons such as:

- to make science more appealing to pupils who enjoy learning in this way;
- to broaden the scope of science, e.g. by looking at how newspapers report developments or crises involving a scientific interpretation;
- to build on pupils' experiences in the primary school, where they will have learnt some of their science by reading textbooks;
- to improve pupils' literacy by providing them with opportunities to study writing in different genres.

There are types of reading activities that go under the heading 'Directed Activities Related to Texts' or DARTs. The driving principle behind these tasks is that pupils should not just be given the text and told to read it but should be asked to do something with it. Simply reading something through may not result in any learning but if the pupil is asked to read the information, think about it and then do something with it then it is more likely that learning will take place. DART-type activities can be done individually or in groups. There are many different types of activities that can be matched to the needs and ability of pupils. The first four activities listed in Figure 5.2 can be described as being DART tasks. Another useful DART exercise involves asking pupils to highlight specific types of information in a text and then to produce some sort of summary, e.g. chart, table, list of bullet points. You will find plenty of other examples in books about teaching (e.g. Parkinson, 1994, pp. 144–51; Ross *et al.*, 2000, pp. 62–7; Centre for Science Education, 1992) and in some textbooks.

Practical activity 5.3

Prepare a DART task for one of your classes. Carefully observe the pupils as they carry it out.

Did you give the pupils sufficient time to read the text and carry out the task?

To what extent did the pupils guess the answers to questions? (They see something in the text that looks as though it might be the answer and put this down without really thinking about it.)

Are there some questions that are trivial or some questions that are too demanding?

Have you devised questions that require pupils to restructure what is written rather than copy it out?

Did the pupils enjoy it?

5   PUPILS WORKING TOGETHER IN GROUPS

Group work provides the opportunity for pupils to talk about the science they know and to express their views or lack of knowledge on any topic you choose. One could argue that we don't give pupils enough time to articulate their understanding of science. In a whole class teaching situation there may be several pupils in a lesson who don't utter even one sentence containing scientific vocabulary. The quieter pupils may feel less threatened and be more willing to express their views when working in a small group than when speaking out in front fo the whole class.

You will find it helpful to direct the groups to produce some thing from their deliberations. This might be an oral contribution from the group's spokesperson to the whole class, or a group-prepared poster, overhead transparency or some other artefact.

In order to focus pupils' attention on the task you will need to give some very clear guidelines about the time for the activity. Some tasks can be short (three to five minutes) – for example when you want to get a quick response to a situation or when you want the pupils to carry out a brainstorming session. When you want pupils to carry out an activity based around some reading or when you want a more substantial product you will need to allow more time, e.g. ten to fifteen minutes.

You may find it helpful to provide the group with some resources to help them to structure their discussion, e.g. a series of questions, or staged outcomes, or you may provide them with some stimulus material, e.g. pictures, apparatus, descriptions of scenarios, video clips. For some discussions you may decide not to provide any structure in order to encourage broader discussion.

| 6 | JIGSAW ACTIVITY |

A jigsaw activity is one where pupils work separately on a particular topic and then bring their expertise back to share with a group and so build up a complete picture of the subject (see Figure 5.4). For example, in a lesson on the electro-magnetic spectrum pupils could be assigned to look at different parts of the spectrum as shown in Figure 5.5. In this situation there are at least three 'experts' working together on any one sub-topic. Their job is to gather together infor-mation from resources provided by the teacher and then to report back to their main group, which will contain experts from all the other sub-topics. You can introduce an element of differentiation into this work by selecting pupils for the different tasks, some of which will be easier than others. You need to think carefully about the information you provide: too much and the pupils will get bogged down, too little and they will simply copy what is there. Pupils will need some guidance – particularly if they are not used to doing this sort of task – such as how to select information and how to present it. You could help them by providing a list of written questions on each topic. Once the experts have prepared information on their topic they return to their main groups where they share it with the others and produce a poster.

| 7 | MAPPING OUT IDEAS IN SCIENCE |

There are a number of different ways of mapping out ideas, two of which are described here. The common feature is the representation of scientific concepts and how they link up to other concepts. They can be used by the teacher for planning and organizing work or by pupils as an aid to thinking things through and for reviewing the extent of their knowledge.

A teacher, or groups of teachers, can use the mapping principle to plan a scheme of work. The key concepts can be written down on pieces of paper and moved around on a planning sheet, giving consideration to the required prior learning and how to build on learning to ensure continuity of the curriculum. Going through this sort of process helps teachers identify potential gaps in pupils' learning and places where concepts are not going to be fully understood if the foundations are not complete.

When using maps in teaching you need to consider:

- when to use them
- how to use them
- what to do with the product.

Mapping pupils' ideas before the start of a topic helps you to get a feeling for what the pupils already know and identifies their misconceptions. The maps can be used as a reference point at the end of a topic. Pupils can then build on it, modify it or completely redo it in a way that helps them to identify their new learning. Alternatively, it can be done solely at the end of the topic to give pupils

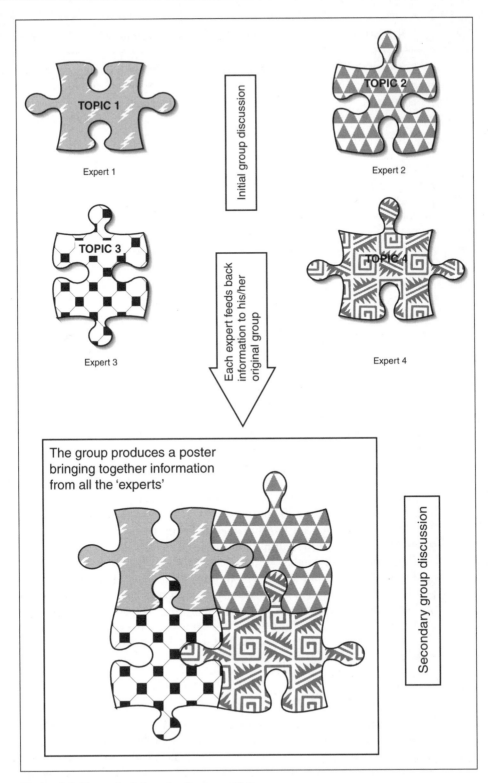

Figure 5.4 *The principles of a jigsaw activity*

Expertise	Group 1	Group 2	Group 3
Whole spectrum	Leanne & Natalie	Stephen & Benn	Allyson
Gamma	Stacey	Matthew	Alicia
X-rays	Gemma	Philip	Sophie
Ultraviolet	Rachel	Nicolas	Leonard
Visible	Kylie	Richard	Samantha
Infrared	Hannah	Craig	Simon
Microwaves	Lydia	Daniel	Louise
Radio waves	Melanie	Dylan	Laura Jane

Figure 5.5 *Task allocation for jigsaw activity*

the opportunity to gather together their thoughts and summarize key ideas. Another possibility is to use the maps as part of a revision programme, perhaps linking together a number of topics.

A great deal of benefit can be gained from doing the mapping exercise in groups. The maps can be built up on the board through a class brainstorming or discussion activity or they can be the product of small group discussion. The concept words can be given to pupils on paper or they can be asked to write them down themselves on the planning sheet. Alternatively, the pupils can be asked to come up with a list of words from the topic they have just been taught. They will need some initial guidance, perhaps working through a few simple maps on the board and then in their books.

The product, in whatever form, can provide the teacher with some useful feedback about the pupils' understanding of the topic. Looking at the links the pupils have made can tell the teacher if the concept has been understood correctly and sometimes the depth of the understanding. Missed, or incorrect, links can give an indication that the work has not been understood. It must be remembered that there is no one correct answer but a good map will contain all the relevant links clearly explained.

7.1 Burr diagrams

Burr diagrams link a key word, usually placed in an oval, with related words surrounding the original word and connected by hooks or burrs. The name is derived from the types of fruits that attach themselves to animals by means of tiny burrs. Pupils can produce these diagrams as a summary at the end of a topic or as a revision aid. Working with the diagram acts as a prompt to think of the

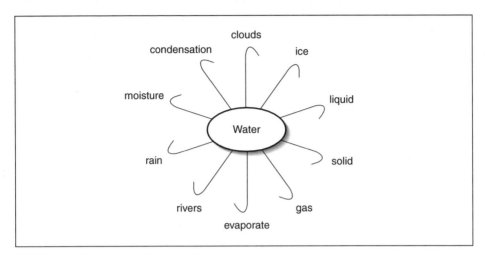

Figure 5.6 *A burr diagram*

connections between the central word and the burr word. Figure 5.6 is typical of a burr diagram produced by a year 7 or year 8 pupil summarizing their work on water. As the pupil learns more about water, e.g. water as a solvent, additional burrs can be added linking the concepts together.

7.2 Concept maps

Concept maps contain more written information than burr diagrams (Figure 5.7). They show the connections between scientific words or concepts, generally written in boxes and called 'objects', though link arrows. The direction of the arrow is important as it helps to show if the concept has been correctly understood. There are five broad types of concept maps of varying degree of difficulty. These can be grouped as follows:

- The pupils have a completely free choice of words from a topic and they use these to construct their own map.
- The pupils are supplied with the words on card and they arrange these themselves and work out the links.
- The objects are arranged on a page and the pupils have to complete the map with link arrows and link phrases.
- The objects and the arrows are provided for the pupils. Only the link phrases have to be added.
- The outline framework is provided along with the link phrases. The pupils have to insert the object words in the boxes. Clues can be given, such as a list of word to choose from or by making the boxes different shapes or colours.

As with other activities in this chapter these can be fun activities and pupils can find themselves talking about science without realizing it. Concept mapping can be done on a computer with the help of specialized software, e.g. Inspiration (for details see *www.inspiration.com*). With this approach it is easy

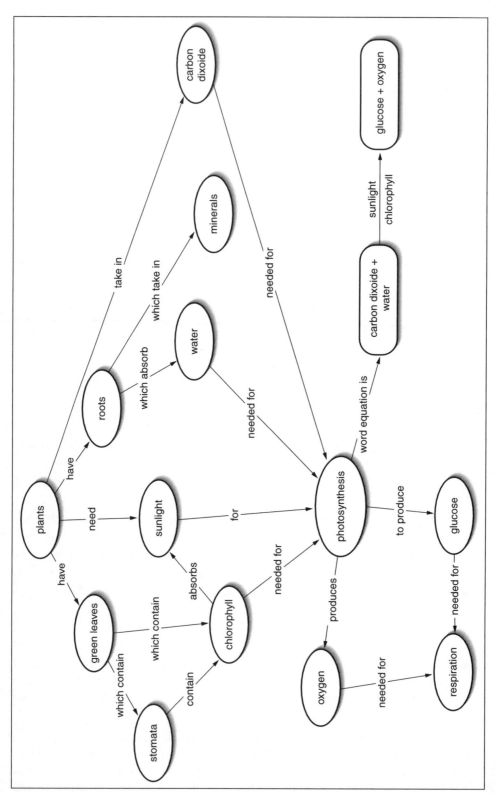

Figure 5.7 *Concept map on plants*

for the pupil to modify and update the concept map and the product is neat and easy to read.

You may wish to give a mark for pupils' concept maps to indicate their level of understanding of the topic. Many of the systems given in the literature are complex and put a great strain on the working memories of the scorers. Kinchin (2000a) suggests a more workable approach where the teacher concentrates on the correctness of the links between the concepts. Marks can be given for:

- the existence of a relationship between the concepts;
- a correct label indicting the relationship;
- correct use of the arrow.

Practical activity 5.4

Consider the pros and cons of carrying out concept mapping exercises in the following ways:

- providing the pupils with key words on paper versus allowing the pupils to come up with a list of words;
- allowing pupils to work in small groups on a concept map over the duration of the teaching of the topic, encouraging them to modify their map as their understanding grows;
- asking pupils to produce a concept map using specialized software on a computer;
- requiring a product that can be displayed versus allowing the pupils to produce a product where neatness is not a major concern;
- asking the pupils to use clipart or newspaper cuttings to illustrate the ideas versus using text only.

8 | CONCEPT CARTOONS

Concept cartoons are simple drawings of a number of individuals with each person making a different statement about the science involved in an everyday situation (Figure 5.8.). The purpose of the cartoon is to promote thinking about science concepts. They can be used for a variety of purposes such as a stimulus for group discussion or a starting point for an investigation. Every situation doesn't necessarily have a 'right answer' and pupils will have to think if they need more information to come to an overall conclusion. Used in this way, pupils can begin to see that not everything in science is certain and what is most important is to look at all the evidence available. A considerable amount of work on this approach to teaching has been carried out by Naylor and Keogh who have produced a resource for teachers containing background information and a large number of concept cartoons (Naylor and Keogh, 2000).

Kinchin (2000b) suggests that a combination of concept cartoons and concept mapping may help in revealing pupils' beliefs and underlying assumptions about

Figure 5.8 *An example of a concept cartoon*

natural phenomena. In his article he takes the example of photosynthesis, a topic where misconceptions abound, and underneath the cartoon places fragments of a concept map which breaks down the words in the speech bubble into manageable chunks. This makes it easier for the pupils to handle during discussion.

9 | MODELLING

Different types of models are used in science, and the benefits of using them to explain phenomena, were described in Chapter 3. Presenting pupils with opportunities to carry out modelling in small groups can be a useful way of helping them to learn. For example, pupils may be asked to carry out a mental modelling task where they are asked to explain something they have observed using their existing knowledge. Using words and/or diagrams each group should come up with a solution. This then opens up the opportunity for a class discussion on the plausibility of these various models. Another approach would be to provide groups with physical- or computer-generated models, ask a series of questions about the validity of the model and then get the pupils to use it to predict what might happen in a new situation.

Practical activity 5.5

What type of model is:

- a slink spring?
- a ball and stick model of a molecule?
- an ionic lattice model?
- a cooling can experiment to study the effects of different types of insulation?

What could you do to prevent pupils from drawing the wrong conclusions from a lesson involving the use of models?

When you teach a lesson that involves the use of a model, carry out the following to check pupils' understanding:

- Ask the pupils to comment on the similarities and differences between the model and reality.
- Ask them to use the model in a new situation. How does the model help to explain the new phenomenon? Have the pupils got sufficient grasp of the model to be able to adapt it?

10 ROLE-PLAY AND DRAMA

Role-play and drama involves the pupils in taking the part of things or other people. It can help pupils to understand phenomena by being actively involved in situations and having to think things through in order to participate. Basically, there are two different types of role-play:

- activities where phenomena are modelled (e.g. pupils depict particle movement in solids, liquids and gases);
- activities where pupils take on the role of a person (for this type of task pupils require a briefing document, outlining the characteristics of the role, but they use their own words when presenting the role).

The modelling type of role-play usually lasts only five to ten minutes. For example, you may wish to teach about energy transfers in electric circuits by asking a group of about ten pupils to be electrons each carrying a packet of energy. The pupils can be arranged in a circle going through 'the battery' and 'a bulb' giving up and receiving energy as appropriate but always keeping the same number of electrons (the current).

The second type of role-play involves a simulation of a particular event and will take up a whole lesson or longer. It is a very good way of getting pupils to appreciate that there is frequently more than one way of looking at a situation. The event might be an enquiry into an environmental issue, looking at the arguments for preserving the environment against the need for materials, energy or land. Or it might be a simulated debate over a scientific issue looking at the evidence to support one theory or another. In an article by McSharry and Jones

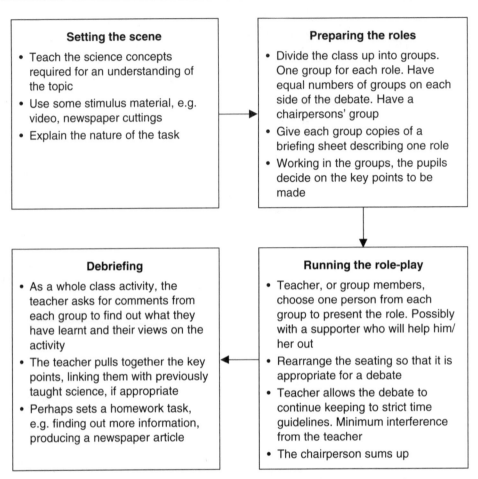

Setting the scene

- Teach the science concepts required for an understanding of the topic
- Use some stimulus material, e.g. video, newspaper cuttings
- Explain the nature of the task

Preparing the roles

- Divide the class up into groups. One group for each role. Have equal numbers of groups on each side of the debate. Have a chairpersons' group
- Give each group copies of a briefing sheet describing one role
- Working in the groups, the pupils decide on the key points to be made

Debriefing

- As a whole class activity, the teacher asks for comments from each group to find out what they have learnt and their views on the activity
- The teacher pulls together the key points, linking them with previously taught science, if appropriate
- Perhaps sets a homework task, e.g. finding out more information, producing a newspaper article

Running the role-play

- Teacher, or group members, choose one person from each group to present the role. Possibly with a supporter who will help him/her out
- Rearrange the seating so that it is appropriate for a debate
- Teacher allows the debate to continue keeping to strict time guidelines. Minimum interference from the teacher
- The chairperson sums up

Figure 5.9 *A possible sequence of events when using role-play to debate an issue*

(2000) containing a number of examples of different types of role-plays the authors point out that it is important to start off with something fairly simple and short before tackling more complex tasks. Some classes of pupils are more open to role-play activities than others. Some pupils feel inhibited because they are shy or because they don't want to show themselves up in front of their peers. If it's not 'cool' they are just not going to do it. Once you have got a good relationship with a class you will be surprised what you can get them to do and once they have got into the routine of the role-play they will enjoy it and learn some science in the process. Figure 5.9 outlines the stages that you should consider going through in planning your activity. When supplying pupils with details of their roles you should provide them with sufficient information to put together a reasonable argument but leave them with the scope to add information and personalize the character.

Drama is slightly different as it gives pupils greater artistic licence. In a drama activity you would provide pupils with a description of the task, a list of the key science concepts, and a list of some techniques that they could consider using. It gives pupils the opportunity to let their imagination run wild and to think about

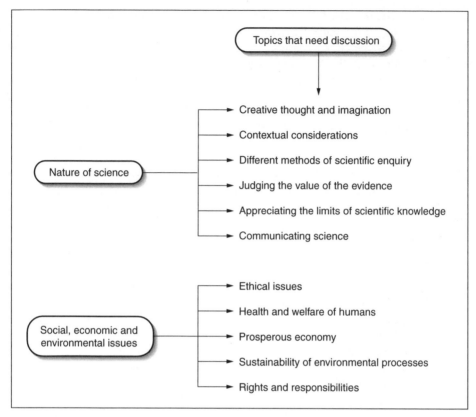

Figure 5.10 *Different strands of teaching ideas and evidence in science*

different ways of depicting things through mime, dance, movement, etc. Braund (1999) in describing the basis for a number of drama activities makes it clear that this sort of approach will not appeal to all pupils, but its inclusion into a science SoW is likely to be of benefit to those who prefer a more creative method of learning.

11 USING SOME OF THESE IDEAS TO TEACH ABOUT IDEAS AND EVIDENCE

The NC requires you to teach about scientific controversies, the contextual framework in which scientific development takes place and social, environmental and ethical issues in science. Figure 5.10 outlines the main strands of work that you need to address. These are things that you may not have studied at all during your time at school or even at university. You may also feel concerned about your lack of knowledge of some of the issues involved. Some topics, such as genetic engineering and global warming are extremely complex in terms of both the science and the ethical issues. In teaching these sorts of topics it is inevitable that you are going to have to make some simplifications in order to make them accessible to your pupils. As long as the simplifications are basically true there is no problem with this – after all, we have to simplify a lot of the science we teach, e.g. structure of the atom, in order for pupils to have a working model to help them explain other phenomena.

You also need to be aware that you are transmitting messages about the nature of science through the way in which you teach and the classroom activities you use. There is a danger that science is presented to pupils as a list of facts to remember in order to pass examinations and this can lead to pupils thinking about science in purely black and white terms. In reality we have a mixture of those things we know for certain and those we don't. Science, particularly chemistry, also has an image problem. Pupils don't see any of our modern conveniences as being associated with science but they do tend to associate environmental problems, etc., back to the interfering scientist. Generally, pupils find it difficult to appreciate the change in lifestyle that has been brought about through scientific development.

Much of our teaching about the nature of science will inevitably be historical, examining how scientists have made progress, the background circumstances that have impinged on the development and the motivational factors involved. You will find information about scientific developments in all modern textbooks and in books specifically written for teaching the nature of science (see examples in Figure 5.11). Introducing stories about real people and the dilemmas they have faced can play a major part in motivating pupils. All too often pupils see science as remote and abstract, giving clear-cut answers. The NC and the GCSE specifications identify opportunities for teaching how scientists use creative thought, and about ethical issues and the responsibilities of citizens.

Ratcliffe (1998) provides some very helpful advice on the procedures that might be followed when discussing socio-scientific issues. These are:

- Make sure that the pupils know why they are doing the activity – for example, this could be couched in terms of looking at the dilemmas scientist have to face when deciding whether or not to do a piece of research.

- Make sure that the pupils have a clear understanding of the relevant science – these activities are not designed to teach science although they may cause misconceptions to come to light.

- Clarification might be required as the discussion progresses – there is nothing wrong with gut reaction based on feelings and personal belief but you will probably want pupils to make decisions based on evidence. In the confines of a classroom discussion the pupils may not be able to go in search of additional information and so you may want to have additional information up your sleeve just in case. You could also discuss with pupils that perhaps all the information isn't available, either it is stored in inaccessible places or it simply doesn't exist.

- Use a framework for the analysis of the discussion – you may find it useful to provide pupils with a list of headings or questions that will guide them through their discussion and help them to come to some sort of conclusions. Also get them to reflect on the process so that they can feed into a whole class debate at the end of the lesson.

- Make sure that pupils aren't put down for expressing their personal views –

you may have to use the 'Ok, that's fine, but have you thought about . . .?' approach.

- Construct the groups so that they work well together – consider using friendship groups but make sure you have a good cross section of skills present. Choose a suitable number to give a variety of views and ensure that everyone has a role.

- Review the activity – make sure that everyone learns from the experience as well as from the outcome of the discussion. Being able to work in a group, recognize other people's points of view and make decisions are very important skills.

Practical activity 5.6

Consider what messages you covey to pupils about the nature of science by doing the following:

- fixing an experiment so that you obtain the 'right' results;
- providing pupils with detailed instructions to carry out an investigation;
- blaming the apparatus for giving the wrong result;
- ignoring modern developments in science because they are not specifically mentioned in the syllabus;
- disallowing debate and discussion over scientific issues because they take up too much teaching time and they leave pupils with a feeling of uncertainty.

How would you convey to your pupils that there are many dimensions to science (some things are certain – others are not, science brings us some benefits but sometimes there are drawbacks)?

For a fuller treatment see Wellington (2000, Chapter 11).

What sort of an image do you want to convey to your pupils about science? How are you going to achieve your goal?

CONCLUSION

The quality of pupils' learning is generally directly proportional to the quality of the teaching they receive. You need to think carefully about the methods you use and consider how they meet or fail to meet the needs of your pupils. When carrying out inspections, members of the Ofsted team will focus their attention on the sorts of things the pupils experience in a lesson. In a recent report (Ofsted, 2001, p. 15) they have provided some examples of activities that lack rigor or depth and lead to situations where the learning is not as good as it should be. In these cases the teacher:

KS	Topic area	Possible teaching approach and resources
3	Vaccination – Jenner's work on smallpox	Group discussion about the scientific processes adopted by Jenner followed by a role-play of a child being used in Jenner's experiments using cowpox. ('Jabs for James Phipps' Solomon, 1990, p. 7).
	Allergies Reactivity of metals	Reading exercise followed by discussion (group or class) and answering questions ('Body piercing', Science Web Reader, 2000, p. 28).
	Geological changes	Reading exercise, class discussion, modelling of rock folding 'Geological changes', Science Web Reader, 2000, p. 43).
	Burning	Practical work and group discussion based on information cards (Warren, 2001b, p. 15).
4	The contribution of Darwin to the development of ideas on evolution	Reading the story of Darwin. Looking at some of the evidence. Group discussion of the development of a theory – how it gains acceptance ('The origin of the species', Ellis, 1992, p. 18).
	The development of ideas about the Solar System	Trial of Galileo – a role-play or group discussion ('The retrial of Galileo', SATIS 16–19, 1990, Unit 1).
	Air pollution	Data analysis, reading, group discussion, role-play ('Is the Earth getting hotter', Science Web Reader: Chemistry, 2000, p. 30); 'Air pollution', The World of Science, 1997, p. 82).
	Plastics	The story of Roy Plunkett and the discovery of Teflon®. Illustrates that some scientific discoveries are made by chance. Reading and answering questions (Warren, 2001b, p. 39).

Figure 5.11 *Examples of activities used to teach the nature of science*

- provides trivial and time-consuming tasks which do not help the pupils to make progress in their understanding of science, e.g. cutting out and sticking pictures on posters;
- pitches work or explanations at the wrong level for the pupils' present understanding;

- uses questioning that is superficial or demands only one word answers;
- use workbooks that limit pupils' responses and constrain the scope and depth of science ideas and awareness of applications;
- tells the pupils what is going to happen in experimental work or ask the pupils to carry out investigations that either have little science content or do not draw on or develop science ideas.

Practical activity 5.7

This chapter contains descriptions of various types of learning activities and Chapter 2 contained descriptions of various types of learners. Take each one of the activities described in this chapter and consider how effective they may be in helping each of the different types of learners in their enjoyment and understanding of science.

CHAPTER 6

Learning science through ICT

Computers have been used in science teaching for the last fifteen years or so, from the early days of the 32K BBC machines to the sophisticated machines we have at present. Over this period a considerable amount of evidence about the ways that Information and Communications Technology (ICT) can promote learning has been collected. Here are a few examples taken from Leask and Pachler (1999, p. 5):

- Pupils who have not enjoyed learning can be encouraged by the use of IT.
- IT gives pupils immediate access to richer source materials.
- IT can present information in new ways which help pupils to understand, assimilate and use it more readily.
- Computer simulations encourage analytical and divergent thinking.
- IT can often compensate for the communication and learning difficulties of pupils with physical and sensory impairment.

The vast majority of pupils enjoy working on computers. There are many reasons for this: they can be fun; they produce work that looks neat; and they can do all sorts of things that can't be done on other media. In my experience many science trainee teachers enjoy working with computers and have a high level of personal competence. Putting these two together has the potential to unleash a vast array of learning opportunities for pupils. But before we take an in-depth look at the learning opportunities offered by IT it is worth bearing in mind a few words of caution:

- Even with the best planning in the world, things can go wrong when using computers. It is a good idea to prepare another activity just in case the computers crash.
- It is unlikely that you will know the ins and outs of every piece of software you use, or the detailed operation of the computer and printer, but make sure that you are technically competent to deal with minor problems.
- Know the capabilities of your computers. You may prepare some material at home or at university using the latest equipment and find that it runs very slowly, or not at all, on the equipment in school.

By the end of this chapter you should:

- understand how computers can be used in science lessons;
- appreciate the importance of the role of the teacher during ICT work;

- be able to decide when to use ICT in your lesson and when it is best to use another teaching technique;
- know how to use ICT for preparation and record keeping.

1 | THE ARRANGEMENTS FOR USING COMPUTERS IN SCIENCE LESSONS

In any one school you will find computers used in a variety of ways depending on what is being taught and what facilities are available. At present, most schools have a number of computer rooms containing machines (usually PCs) that are networked together. In addition they may have stand-alone machines in other teaching rooms. However, the ICT provision in schools is changing very rapidly and as the cost of equipment, such as data projectors and CD-writers, comes down in price we are likely to see a growing amount of sophisticated equipment in classrooms. Three different approaches to work using computers with classes are described below:

- the electronic blackboard (teacher in control of the keyboard);
- working in the computer room (individual pupils in control of the keyboard);
- working on computers in the science laboratory (individuals or groups of pupils in control of the keyboard).

1.1 The electronic blackboard approach

The blackboard or whiteboard will always be with us. It plays a key role in helping pupils to learn by providing a medium for carrying out such jobs as jotting down important points or building links between concepts as the lesson progresses. But an increasing number of schools are also using an electronic blackboard approach. One way of doing this is to simply link a computer to a large monitor or TV using the normal coaxial or SCART lead. Alternatively, the image can be shown on a screen by linking the computer to a data projector. The teacher can then work with the class using images from the computer. For example, the teacher can:

- work through some aspects of a CD-ROM, showing snippets of video or simulation and pausing to ask the pupils questions;
- explain how to use a particular piece of software;
- go through downloaded websites and discuss how the information can be used;
- use presentational software such as PowerPoint.

The use of PowerPoint opens up a number of opportunities for teachers, such as:

- the preparation of slides that are attractive and motivating for pupils;
- the inclusion of web pages and video clips;

- the possibility of giving pupils miniaturized copies of the slides as handouts;
- the possibility of modifying the slides to cater for the needs of different groups of pupils;
- the possibility of providing pupils with an electronic copy of the presentation if they wish to work through it on their own.

PowerPoint is clearly good at presenting information in an attractive manner. The structure of the package tends to guide the writer in a way that results in presentations that are set out in a logical, concise and straightforward way. One of the drawbacks of using this method is that it tends to foster a didactic approach to teaching and, if you are not careful, you end up giving a lecture rather than an interactive lesson. When using PowerPoint you need to think about how you are going to pause and break up the presentation and how you are going to involve the pupils.

A further development of the electronic blackboard is the use of an interactive screen such as a SMART board. This allows the teacher to add to the image on the screen using different coloured 'electronic pens', rub things out and use the touch-sensitive nature of the surface of the screen to change the display.

1.2   Using the computer room

In the main, pupils work by themselves on a computer in the computer room. In this way pupils work at their own pace and, to a certain extent, can interact with the software in ways that suit them. Using this approach opens up the possibilities of providing pupils with differentiated learning. For example:

- different tasks can be given to different groups of pupils in the class;
- pupils could be directed to work through different parts of a CD-ROM package;
- pupils could get through the work at different rates (differentiation by outcome).

There are a number of management issues that need to be considered when working with pupils in this way. The first is concerned with shifting the pupils' attention from the computer to you as teacher. This is likely to happen at least once during the lesson, at the start when you want to introduce the task, but will probably happen two or three times when you want to pull things together or get the pupils to move on. During these times it is important that the pupils' attention is focused on the teacher and that they face the teacher rather than the computer. The second is concerned with keeping the pupils on task. You may find that pupils want to look at other things on the computer system or they may want to try out some new procedure – the '*I just want to see if this works*' stance. One of your aims may be for the pupils to develop their IT skills and you would, therefore, want them to do some experimenting with the technology but, hopefully, the key focus of your lesson would be concerned with learning science and you would want them to concentrate on the planned activities. The third issue is to do with timing. If you have gone to the trouble of booking the computer room you may feel that pupils should spend all of the lesson time interacting with the computer. In some instances that may be fine but frequently this approach may be unproductive in terms of pupils' learning. This may involve breaking up the task into smaller units or the use of different computer features, e.g. pupils may access information from a CD-ROM or website and then write some notes using the word processor.

It is worth bearing in mind that you might be able to get extra science ICT time by liaising with the IT teacher. She/he might be looking around for some meaningful contexts in which pupils can develop their IT skills. Working alongside the IT teacher could benefit both of you.

You may be aware that pupils frequently have difficulty in transferring information from one subject area to another. For example, they may well have learnt how to carry out particular functions in mathematics but they find it difficult to use these skills in their science lessons. A similar problem can occur with science lessons carried out in the computer room and science lessons carried out in the laboratory. You will need to consider how you can integrate the work carried out in the two locations by methods such as bringing the product from the computer-based lesson into the laboratory or by providing the pupils with a number of verbal cross-references.

1.3 Using computers in the science laboratory

An increasing number of schools have a small number of computers situated in science laboratories. There are a number of ways of organizing pupils to work in this situation, such as:

- including the computer(s) as part of a circus of activities (groups of pupils rotate round the different tasks);
- allowing pupils to access the computers for information as and when they need it (e.g. as one of a number of resources in the room required for completion of a task or adding experimental results to a database or spreadsheet in order to produce a class set);
- arranging groups of pupils around each computer (dependent on the number of pupils and class size);
- planning for groups to work on different tasks, some of which need computers and some of which don't (towards the end of the lesson pupils could pool ideas that they have learnt from the different sources);
- using computers for extension or remedial work (pupils could access more difficult tasks on the computer or they may go there for help).

Practical activity 6.1

You may find that some science teachers prefer working in the IT room whereas others are quite content to use the computers in the science laboratory. Some schools have a mini IT suite shared between all the science laboratories. What are the advantages and disadvantages of these different arrangements. Consider both teacher organization and pupils' learning.

2 | PUPILS' LEARNING

Pupils are keen to work on computers. In fact it is sometimes difficult to get them to stop work and move them on to some other activity. But how does all this work lead to pupils improving their knowledge of science? To a large extent this depends on the type of activity that pupils are involved in so in this section we will look at a few examples.

2.1 The computer as teacher

Many science CD-ROMs are designed to teach pupils specific science topics. They teach the pupil by providing explanations and some activities and end up by asking a few questions. Should the pupil get the questions wrong she/he is directed back to the part of program that taught the topic. There are similarities in the teaching approach used by this type of program and the way that a classroom teacher operates but there are significant differences. The computer cannot:

- offer alternative explanations;
- deal with additional problems and any side issues the pupils may have.

2.2 Supporting pupils' thinking by using a computer

In some instances a computer can help to simplify situations or provide support to help pupils' learn, thus allowing the pupil to spend more time on certain key aspects of the science. For example, by using data logging equipment the pupil does not have to worry about taking the measurements and can concentrate on the manipulation of the data. Another example is the use of spreadsheets to plot histograms, line graphs and pie charts without requiring the pupils to do complex calculations. In this context the computer is acting as a support for the pupils' learning, as it reduces the overall amount of information the pupils have to deal with. This is an example of the process called 'scaffolding' mentioned on page 23 but this time it is a machine that is giving the support rather than another person (Kennewell et al., 2000).

Pupils can learn from the process of having to express their ideas on paper The act of composing a piece of writing requires the pupil to think through the work carefully and make sure that the reasoning is correct. For example, pupils might be asked to explain the results of an experiment. Some pupils will get it all right first time round but there will be others who will sequence their arguments incorrectly or miss out important pieces of information. Using the traditional pen and paper approach means that the whole piece has to be rewritten but with a word processor a simple redrafting is all that is required.

2.3 Collaborative learning with computers

Pupils will frequently work in groups around the computer. This situation provides opportunities for group discussion about science. While going round the groups you may hear pupils say things like:

http://www.rtweb.info

- 'I never really saw it that way before' (throwing new light on a previously understood concept);

- 'Are you sure that's right?' (checking personal understanding);

- 'Let's try that and see if it works' (the trial and error approach).

The computer acts as a focus for the discussion and frequently helps to keep pupils on task. Collaborative writing is a good way of getting pupils to articulate their science knowledge and it has the advantage of leading to a product that can be easily analysed by the teacher (Scrimshaw, 1993).

Practical activity 6.2

Carry out a study of the interactions that go on between pupils while they are working on a computer program. You could do this by observing a group or by tape recording their conversations (with their permission) or by asking them to jot down what they talked about. Clearly the fact that you are showing an interest in what they are doing will have some effect on their actions but the exercise will give you some feedback on the type of conversations that go on. You should look for use of science vocabulary (correct and incorrect), reasoning and how decisions are made.

The types of learning described above will only take place if the teacher plans out the activities carefully and provides appropriate support during the lesson. This may involve making suggestions that they look at other resources or tackle a slightly different problem depending on their level of success with the initial task.

2.4 Extended learning through the web

Information has never been so easy to obtain. Through the Internet and the World Wide Web pupils have access to a wealth of science sites, opening up the possibility of boundless learning. Some pupils are likely to take advantage of this opportunity and extend their learning well beyond the work covered in the classroom. This is not a new problem as there have always been a few individuals who want to find out more. However, learning from the computer is likely to be an area that will increase considerably over the next decade or so and you may wish to consider how you are going to:

- help pupils locate science sites where you can be sure that the science is correct;

- help pupils evaluate science sites for bias, e.g. environmental organizations, manufacturing companies, government sites;

- equip pupils with the skills to search for information;

- equip pupils with the skills to extract information from the sites and move their learning along.

As teachers you should be providing pupils with the skills they require for lifelong learning. You want them to enjoy learning and to go on finding things out for themselves once the support of the teacher is no longer available. This independent learning will involve them using a variety of media but, increasingly, information is likely to be transmitted in electronic form.

Many pupils have computers at home, opening up the possibility of different types of home-based learning. In a recent report it was said that 80 per cent of upper income families and 53 per cent of lower income families had a computer at home (Facer *et al.*, 2000). You may find that in some of your classes all the pupils will have computers at home. While we have a mixed situation it is not possible to move entirely to electronic homework, but here are a couple of ideas that are worth considering:

- Notes and exercises are given to pupils either on disk or by email. Pupils can go over the work in their own time and carry out the exercises, which can be printed out and handed in for marking. The pupil can easily make corrections on the electronic version to ensure that s/he has an accurate set of answers.

- Teachers can ask pupils to find out information from electronic encyclopaedias or websites and bring this back to the classroom for discussion.

Practical activity 6.3

Examine the SoW for a year group and note when ICT is used. Cross-check the activities with the lesson objectives and comment on the match. Are there other topics in the SoW where the use of ICT would be profitable?

Pupils can learn using computers at home or those in the school library or open access IT suite. Try to find out to what extent this is used by different subject groups within the school. What sort of tasks are appropriate for this type of learning? What are your views on providing pupils with their notes on disk? To what extent is the school's policy on ICT changing as the technology improves?

3 | USING THE INTERNET AND WORLD WIDE WEB

The Internet and the web provides teachers and pupils with a vast amount of information and resources, so much in fact that individuals can become overwhelmed. It is all too easy to get sidetracked when searching or to spend time looking at material that turns out to be irrelevant. What follows gives an indication of what the web can offer, and gives you some guidance as to how to maximize the learning and minimize the time spent on searching.

3.1 Finding suitable sites for pupils to use

You will very quickly build up a list of suitable sites for pupils to access but a good start is to go to well-established UK sites such as the NGfL, BECTa and

www.dfes.gov.uk/index.htm	DfES
www.wales.gov.uk/polinfo/education/education_e.htm	National Assembly – Education (Wales)
www.becta.org.uk/index.cfm	BECTa – advice and help about using ICT in schools
http://vtc.ngfl.gov.uk/resource/cits/science/ideas.html	Ideas for using ICT in science teaching
www.ofsted.gov.uk	Ofsted and inspection reports
www.canteach.gov.uk/home.htm	Teacher Training Agency
www.ase.org.uk/	Association for Science Education
www.rsc.org www.chemsoc.org	The Royal Society of Chemistry
www.iop.org/	Institute of Physics
www.iob.org/	Institute of Biology

Figure 6.1 *Some useful websites (note that website addresses may change from time to time)*

ASE sites. These will lead you on to sites that are appropriate for the National Curriculum and post-16 work.

Printed worksheets containing web addresses, together with teachers' notes, are available at, for example, the ASE and BECTa websites (Sang, 2000b; BECTa, 2000). Textbooks and books about teaching now include web-based science activities, e.g. de Cicco *et al.* (1998).

Reviews of websites are published in journals, magazines and newspapers such as School Science Review, the TES and Education in Chemistry. Figure 6.1 lists the addresses of a number of useful sites both for teaching purposes and for keeping up to date on educational issues.

3.2   Getting the pupils to log on to the site

Clearly pupils can type in the web addresses for themselves but they frequently make mistakes and you can save them a lot time and frustration by providing the addresses on disk or through the school's intranet. You may find it useful to build up a selection of useful site addresses as Word documents under topic headings. You can then select from your list and mail these to pupils. There may be times when you want to give the pupils a fairly free rein and let them carry out a search but it would be unwise to do this without a prior discussion on search techniques.

3.3 Ways of using sites

One of the things to consider during the planning stage is the number of sites you want the pupils to work on. You will find that it is better to limit the work to a small number of sites to avoid overloading the pupils with information. If they have too many sites they will start to forget where they saw things and will waste time flicking backwards and forwards.

You also need to think about how you are going to maintain pupils' attention while they are working on-line. If the task is too long, or the content of the sites too complicated, pupils will switch off. Pupils may tend to skip quickly through long sections of writing and not fully understand what is being said. You may find it helpful to provide pupils with worksheets containing questions that require them to extract information from the sites and compose a report of their own. These may be in the usual written form or may be interactive guides, where the instructions are web pages themselves.

The aim of the lesson might be to gather information about a particular topic and write a report about it. Pupils may print information from the web pages or make notes for use at a later date. They may cut out information and paste it into their own document. However, simple movement of information form one place to another is not going to help the pupils to learn at all. It is far more profitable to get the pupils to use the information to compose something themselves.

You may find that some teachers think that using computers in this way is more or less a waste of time. They would argue that it takes a great deal of effort to book the computer room and that all that the pupils are doing is finding out information which they can find in books or the teacher can tell them. If they are really 'anti-computer' they will also talk about the unreliability of the machines and how can you stop pupils going on to other sites. The justification for using the web can be based around the following arguments:

- Pupils can carry out a piece of authentic research by asking questions of scientists or going to sites that contain up to date information, e.g. the NASA site, sites containing information on earthquakes, energy use, endangered species, weather.

- There are opportunities for exchanging information about science with others within the school and other pupils throughout the world (see Science Across the World below) and thus help to create a positive global culture for learning science. This can be done through the school or other website, or by email.

- Not all information is easy to find by traditional means. Frequently information can be retrieved more quickly using the web than by searching through books in a library. This could be of use when pupils are studying the work of scientists.

- Directing pupils to newspaper, radio and television sites can help to draw their attention to current issues in science such as global warming, health issues, GM crops, etc. Using the Internet enables the pupils to look at a number of different reports on the same issue and draw comparisons.

- Pupils can download pictures and clipart that can be used to enhance their written reports. This isn't as trivial as it might first appear as it is all part of encouraging pupils to take pride in their work and promoting an interest in science.

3.4 Science Across the World (SAW)

The web can do a lot to broaden pupils' horizons in discovering that pupils in different parts of the world have the same sorts of concerns as they have. Communicating with pupils in other countries can help to develop a scientific culture within a school and an awareness of global needs. Many schools have set up links with other schools but the link does not always extend to the science department.

 The ASE, in conjunction with BP, run a project called Science Across the World where pupils in different countries work on a particular topic and exchange the information they have collected (www.ase.org.uk/sworld.html). For example, the information could be:

- the results of experiments carried out in the school;

- the results of a survey;

- a review of what the country or the school is doing with regard to an environmental issue.

The schools involved use materials from one of the SAW units published by the ASE. Each unit focuses on an issue of common concern, e.g. drinking water, food, energy, global warming and health, but takes into account the wide regional variations. The unit packs contain information for teachers and pupils written in different languages. There is no compulsion to exchange information by electronic means but it saves on time and cost.

3.5 Working offline

In some circumstances you may decide that it is best to work offline. This may be to do with cost or you may be worried that the line could go down during the lesson and ruin your plan. In order to do this you will need to download the sites yourself, saving them either in html format or as a Word document. While this will restrict what you can do it does mean you can work with the pages on any computer containing the appropriate software and you don't have to be in a room that is linked to the Internet. The procedure for doing this and for producing a hyperlinked electronic worksheet is given in Figure 6.2.

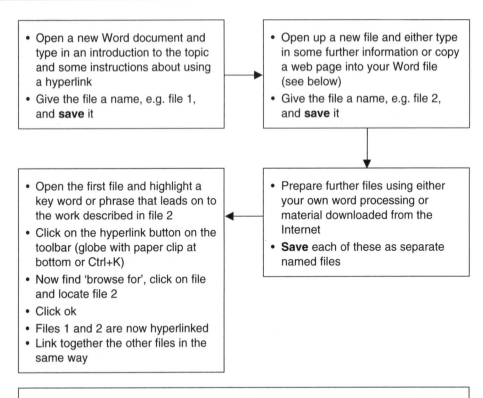

Downloading web pages is easy through Office 2000 and can be accomplished by pressing the appropriate button. Downloading using earlier versions of Office requires you to select sections of text and artwork and copy them separately. When you have downloaded the files into Word you should remove the original hyperlinks.

Figure 6.2 *Preparing a hyperlinked worksheet*

Practical activity 6.4

Prepare an electronic worksheet for the pupils using two to four websites. Consider how you are going to focus pupils' attention on these sites rather than allowing them to carry out a wider search.

4 USING MULTIMEDIA

Multimedia refers to programs that present information using more than one medium, e.g. printed words and video clips. These are found mainly in CD-ROM format but are increasingly becoming available on the web. To a certain extent some of these packages have replaced the use of traditional videos in lessons as it is possible to quickly select the appropriate piece of video and to repeat the play as many times as necessary. However, the quality of some videos is poor and the size of the image is sometimes quite small.

Some multimedia programs, or parts of programs, readily lend themselves to whole class teaching using a large monitor or data projector. You will have to select which parts you are going to use and how you are going to build your lesson around these sequences. You need to avoid showing long sequences of text, which is likely to result in pupils switching off, and running sequences that are presented at a level that is beyond the capabilities of the pupils. Other multimedia programs are better used on a one-to-one or small group basis. These sometimes include quiz questions and reward the pupils for a correct answer with a numerical score. Although some teachers may use these programs to teach the topic I suspect that in the vast majority of cases they are used to supplement other classroom activities or as a revision aid at the end of the topic. Some multimedia CD-ROMs are advertised as providing self-tuition and revision courses.

Pupils may be motivated to work on multimedia packages because they can offer:

- attractive colour presentation;
- amusing cartoon characters;
- clear and precise details and explanations;
- the option of producing printed notes;
- animated graphics, including the ability to rotate objects through three dimensions;
- immediate feedback on their understanding.

Pupils tend not to like software when:

- it is directed at a different age group (either too childish or too difficult);
- it is difficult to operate;
- it requires them to go all the way back to the beginning of a sequence if they have only made one error;
- there is a large amount of text to read.

Some multimedia packages contain simulations of scientific processes or present models of situations and phenomena. These can help the pupil to understand by being directly focused on the issue and by working through the arguments in a logical sequence. The static images found in books are replaced by moving sequences which can give a much clearer picture of what happens in reality. Figure 6.3 gives an indication of types of simulations that are available. They cover things that can be done in the laboratory and things that occur on both the atomic scale and the cosmic scale. It would be a sad day if the only experience pupils had of experimental work was through laboratory simulations. Simulations, by their very nature, tend to simplify things and give the impression that things fit together perfectly and experiments always give us the 'right' result. We know that science isn't like that and that a lot can be learnt from the manipulation of the apparatus and looking to see if the results fit the predicted pattern. Science is generally not as 'black and white' as the simulation packages tend to show. Another problem is that pupils sometimes have difficulty in distinguishing between the simulation and reality and you may find it worthwhile

Type of simulation	Title of CD-ROM and publisher
Electrolysis and ion movement	*Electrochemistry* (New Media, www.new-media.co.uk
Simulated experiments	*Crocodile Chemistry* (Crocodile clips, www.crocodile-clips.com)
Flights around the planets	*Atlas of the Solar System* (Dorling Kindersley, www.dk.com/uk
Moving objects	*Investigating Forces and Motion* (Granada Learning, www.granada-learning.com
Parts of the body	*The Ultimate Human Body* (Dorling Kindersley, www.dk.com/uk)
Simulating investigations	*Science Investigations* (Focus Education Software, www.focuseducational.com)
Conserving energy	*Energy House* (Science Online, www.scienceonline.co.uk)
Covers a range of experiments	*Biology Simulations* (AVP, www.avp.co.uk)

Figure 6.3 *CD-ROMs that include simulations*

drawing pupils' attention to the factors that the simulation has not taken into account. Many of the things that were only available on CD-ROMs a few years ago, e.g. video, interactive quizzes, are now available on websites and it may be worthwhile doing a little searching before spending a lot of money on a CD.

Practical activity 6.5

Evaluate the quality of a science CD-ROM in terms of its educational value for a particular year group using the following parameters:

- How easy is it to navigate the different topics on the CD?
- Is the material presented at a suitable level for the age and ability of the group you want to use it with?
- Is the material presented in an attractive way?
- How will pupils react to the speech used on the CD (nature of the voice, level of the language, etc.)?
- In what ways does the material challenge the pupils' thinking?
- Is the CD free of technical problems?
- Compare the learning experiences offered by a CD-ROM with written materials on the same topic.

5 | USING SPREADSHEETS

It is most likely that pupils will be taught about how to use spreadsheets in their core ICT lessons. Science provides pupils with authentic examples of spreadsheet use through the collection of data from experiments and by providing opportunities to use mathematical modelling. Pupils need to think of spreadsheets as a tool to help them understand science and simplify situations. The time to stop using them is when the complexity of the spreadsheet hides or confuses the concepts you are trying to get across to your pupils. In a number of the examples that follow the data can be handled using pen and paper and in some cases this approach would be used in preference to using a computer – but I would argue that learning to use spreadsheets within the context of science is an important skill and pupils need a variety of opportunities to practice this skill.

5.1 Using data from experiments

At the very simplest level pupils could use a spreadsheet to calculate the average value from a set of experimental results. They could move on to applying a formula to the results to calculate a derived variable and look at changes in the data by plotting one variable against another. Spreadsheets really come into their own when a data-logger is used. The software that is used with the data-logger frequently allows the user to transfer the results to a spreadsheet where it can be easily manipulated and displayed graphically.

5.2 Using data from other sources

There is plenty of other data available for teachers to use from the information on the back of food products through to information in books and on web pages. You may start to build up a library of data sets for pupils to use. You need to avoid situations where pupils have to type in large amounts of data themselves as this is not going to add to their learning.

5.3 Mathematical modelling

In this context spreadsheets are used to look at what would happen if you change variables, or change a formula, to the outcome of a situation. Pupils could be asked to model the relationship between surface area and volume, perhaps related to heat loss from animals. Another example would be to model the energy used by a fictitious individual during a day, using values for energy required for various activities such as running, walking, reading and sleeping. This could then be linked to another modelling spreadsheet looking at energy values of different foods. The two could then be matched up to look at what sort of diet might match each individual. Examples of mathematical models are given in Figure 6.4 along with examples of software that uses representational models.

Model	Source
Interrelationship between population of wolves and deers using a spreadsheet	Frost (2000) pp. 38 & 82
Home insulation using a spreadsheet	Frost (2000) pp. 45 & 52
Boyle's law using a spreadsheet	Frost (2000) pp. 44 & 90
Volume to surface area – modelling heat loss from animals and respiration in plants using a spreadsheet	Frost (2000) pp. 68 & 77
Molecular modelling	*Bonding H: Molecular Bonding and Shape* (CyberEd/REM www.r-c-m.co.uk)
Particle movement	*States of Matter* (New Media, www.new-media.co.uk)
Life processes	*Creatures 2* (Mindscape, http://creatures.mindscape.com)

Figure 6.4 *Examples of modelling using a computer*

5.4 Ways of using spreadsheets

You will have to make a judgement about your pupils' ability to cope with spreadsheets based on your conversations with the pupils and the ICT co-ordinator. A good level to start at is to provide the class with something already entered on the spreadsheet. For example, where you want pupils to have practice in writing formulae and producing graphs, you may have already input the initial data in the first two or three columns of the sheet. Because this approach involves the use of relatively simple spreadsheet skills, the teacher can concentrate on helping the pupils to learn the science. Two examples of this type of use are given in Figure 6.5a.

A second way of using spreadsheets is to set up the rows and columns, including the formulae, on a computer in the laboratory and ask pupils to enter data from their experiments once they have obtained it. In this way a class set of results can be obtained and averages calculated. The advantages and disadvantages of working in this way can be discussed with the class. It may be that groups of pupils are working on different aspects of the same experiment or they may be monitoring the experiment in different ways. In these cases a number of spreadsheets could be set up that could be examined by all members of the class, giving an opportunity to compare the different techniques.

A third approach is to require the pupils to build up the spreadsheet themselves. The data could either be from their own practical investigation or

	A	B	C	D	E
1	Electrical item	Power rating (W)	Price of electricity (p/kWh)	Cost of running for 1h (p)	Cost of running for 24h (£.p)
2	light bulb	100	6.65	= (B2/1000)*C2	= D2*24/100
3	low energy bulb	18	**Copy down**	**Copy down**	**Copy down**
4	TV	200			
5	kettle	2500			
6	computer	300			
7	electric fire	2000			
8	hair dryer	1800			
9	vacuum cleaner	500			

	A	B	C	D
1	Planet	Surface gravity relative to Earth	Weight of football (N)	My weight (N)
2	Earth	1	4.5	380
3	Mercury	0.38	=4.5*B3	=380*B3
4	Venus	0.90	**Copy down**	**Copy down**
5	Mars	0.38		
6	Jupiter	2.64		
7	Saturn	1.16		
8	Uranus	1.17		
9	Neptune	1.2		

Figure 6.5 *Examples of spreadsheets (a) Spreadsheets requiring pupils to input simple formulae*

building together data obtained from a number of different sources. For example, when pupils carry out an experiment to determine the formula of magnesium oxide by burning a known mass of magnesium in air, they will initially discuss the problems of accuracy of results and how to calculate the value. They could then look at how a spreadsheet could be used to deal with the data and hopefully come up with something like the sheet shown in Figure 6.5b.

The number of opportunities for using spreadsheets and the complexity of the formulae increases substantially in post-16 science studies. It is with topics such as chemical equilibria, radioactive decay and population dynamincs that pupils really appreciate their value. Further examples of spreadsheet exercises can be found in the book by Tebbutt and Flavell (1995) and in a special edition of *School Science Review* (1997) devoted to the use of ICT in science.

	A	B	C	D	E	F	G	H	I
1	Group	Mass of crucible (g)	Mass of crucible + magnesium (g)	Mass of crucible + magnesium oxide (g)	Mass of magnesium (g)	Mass of oxygen (g)	Moles of magnesium (g)	Moles of oxygen (g)	Ratio of moles of magnesium: moles of oxygen
2	Baz & Chris	27.201	27.354	27.443	=C2-B2	=D2-C2	=E2/24	=F2/16	=G2/H2
3					Copy down	Copy down	Copy down	Copy down	Copy down
4									
5									

Figure 6.5 (b) Determination of the formula of magnesium oxide

6 USING DATABASES

A database is simply a collection of information in a logical form. Pupils will probably be familiar with the terms given to the various parts of a database such as those given in Figure 6.6 from their ICT lessons but, if not, they will need a brief introduction as to how a database is structured. It is useful for pupils to be able to construct simple databases on information they compile themselves and to interrogate larger databases. When the data is purely numeric it is probably best to use a spreadsheet program to organize the data, but when it is alphanumeric or a mixture of data types then a database should be used. By using databases, pupils can see the importance of storing information in a systematic way and to be able to search for patterns. Because of the time it takes to input data, pupils are unlikely to produce very sophisticated databases. They could be used during the course of teaching a topic or at the end when the pupils could be asked to summarize what they have learnt under various field headings. Examples of topics that lend themselves to the production of databases are given in Figure 6.7. You need to bear in mind that pupils might be sensitive about collecting certain forms of information about themselves. For example, pupils are very conscious about being the smallest or the tallest in the class and the fattest or the thinnest. You need to think of variables that are not going to upset anyone, such as those mentioned in the table.

Large databases are available in CD format or on the web and these can be used by pupils to research topics and draw conclusions. Pupils can access up-to-date information on energy consumption, the availability of natural resources and a range of environmental issues. They can study the properties of elements and compounds, look at scientific discoveries over time and get detailed information on planets and moons in our solar system. Pupils will need to develop their searching techniques, e.g. the use of wildcards, and logical (AND – NOT – OR) commands, and consider how best to present their findings. They will need

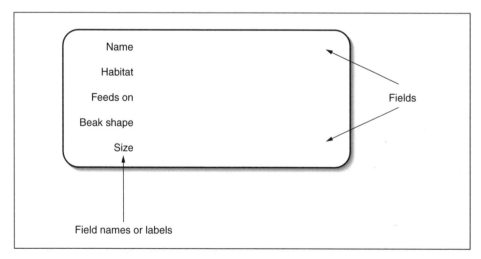

Figure 6.6 *An example of a single record in a database file on birds*

Topic	Breakfast cereals	Members of the class	Planets	Halogens	Plants
	Name	Name	Name	Name	Name
	Carbohydrate content g/100g	Eye colour	Atmosphere	State at room temperature	Colour of flower
	Protein content g/100g	Hair colour	Mass	Colour	Shape of flower
Examples of fields	Energy kJ/100g	Shoe size	Distance from sun	Electronic configuration	Number of petals
	Cost p/100g	Sex	Surface temperature K	Reaction with potassium bromide	Shape of leaves

Figure 6.7 *Examples of suitable topics where pupils can construct their own databases*

to be able to make judgements on the reasonableness, validity and reliability of their findings.

Practical activity 6.6

Select a database that would be useful in your teaching and consider how you are going to structure the activities associated with the topic. Start off with some simple questions that will involve the retrieval of information, e.g. 'How many . . .?' 'Which . . .?' You may go on to questions that require pupils to use more sophisticated sorting tools such as accessing information within ranges. If appropriate you could then ask pupils to look at trends or to make predictions from the data.

7 USING DATA LOGGING

Data logging is used to collect information from experiments over very short periods of time to very long periods of time. To carry out this type of work you need a sensor and an interface. With most, if not all modern, equipment you can collect the data with these two pieces of equipment either in the laboratory or outside the school. The interface device will contain batteries and the experimental data will be stored on a chip. The data can then be transferred to a computer using a suitable lead and software that is compatible with the interface. Each

Sensor/*probe* type	Examples of experiments
Thermometer	Measuring temperature change in chemical reactions. Measuring temperature changes as substances are heated or cooled.
Light sensor	Measuring the rate of reaction when the reaction produces a precipitate. Determining the inverse square law.
Light gates	Measuring speed, time and acceleration.
Sound	Examining sound waves.
Humidity	Determination of transpiration rates.
Position	Monitors the movement of pendulum. When attached to the plunger of a gas syringe it can monitor the volume of gas liberated.
Rotation	Measures speed of rotation.
Pressure	Measures the increase in pressure in a liquid as the depth increases.
pH	Acid-base titrations.
Oxygen	Monitoring ecosystems.
Conductivity	Acid-base titrations. Monitoring the rate of reaction when their is a change in ion concentration.
Radioactive decay	Monitoring radioactive decay using a Geiger tube.

Figure 6.8 *Outline of experiments that can be monitored using data-logging equipment*

educational supplier produces their own loggers and set of sensors that matches their software so once a school has decided on a particular system they are likely to stick to it.

Figure 6.8 gives a number of examples of experiments where data-logging equipment can be used. When certain variables (written in italic in Figure 6.8) are to be measured it is necessary to connect a suitable probe to the relevant meter and connect the meter to the interface. It is possible to monitor two or three variables at any one time by attaching the appropriate sensors to the interface.

As well as being a labour-saving device, data loggers can take a lot of what is referred to as 'noise' (p. 116) out of the experiment, allowing the pupil to concentrate on the results. However, this is only true if the pupil hasn't got to deal with complex software and the intricacies of where to put various leads. You will have to make decisions about what data to collect (both in terms of range and numbers of variables) and how this meets the needs of your pupils.

Practical activity 6.7

Take a simple experiment that can be followed by both traditional means and by using a data logger, e.g. monitoring the drop in temperature as water cools in cans covered with different numbers of layers of insulation. What are the advantages and disadvantages of each method? Take an experiment that couldn't be followed by traditional means, e.g. the production of oxygen during photosynthesis over a weekend. What is the best method of presenting this vast amount of data? What conclusions would you expect the pupils to draw about the methodology?

8 USING A WORD PROCESSOR OR DESK-TOP PUBLISHING PACKAGE

The most common use of word processors by pupils at present is the writing up of investigations for GCSE assessment purposes. But this is just one of a number of ways that word processors can be used to help pupils to learn science. Many of the writing activities described in Chapter 4 can be adapted for use on the computer. Here are a few examples.

8.1 Sequencing activities

Pupils are given a piece of text with the sections jumbled up so that they are not in a sequence that makes sense. The pupils' job is to rearrange the text on screen so that it makes sense and is scientifically correct.

In designing such tasks it is worth considering the following:

- making sure that the task is not so simple that it can be done in a few minutes;
- how you lay out the text so that pupils don't have formatting difficulties when trying to rearrange it;
- including clues in the text to guide them towards the correct sequence;
- how to promote group discussion (e.g. through your introductory remarks about the task, including statements that require pupils to use previously learned science);
- using additional activities (e.g. questions on the text produced, tasks based on further information).

A related exercise is to present pupils with a series of statements, some of which are scientifically correct and some of which are not. The pupils have to correct the statements or add to the statements to make them make sense. This is a good exercise for checking on pupils' understanding and will result in a product that should be useful for revision purposes.

8.2 Writing for different audiences

This involves pupils writing letters, producing posters and newspaper articles. These word processor-based writing tasks have a number of advantages over their pen and paper equivalents. Clearly the overall quality of presentation will be enhanced in the typed format, but there are other benefits of using the computer:

- Artwork can be easily incorporated (clipart, scanned images, images from a digital camera, etc.);
- the text can easily be changed as the group discussion about the topic develops;
- layout devices (e.g. letter frames, columns) can help to make the final product look more professional;
- sections of writing from the web or CD-ROM can be incorporated into the article and commented on (e.g. 'In his report in the Daily News, Marvin Smith says (quote) but our investigations show . . .');
- statistics from the web or CD-ROM can be incorporated into the article and commented on;
- work produced by one group can be easily circulated to other groups in the class for comment;
- the process opens up the opportunity for sending these types of articles to pupils in other schools, possibly in different countries.

When pupils are going to write using information from another source they will need some guidance about how to select what is important. Without help they are likely to copy large chunks of the material. If the information is in printed form you can ask them to read it through carefully and highlight the key features. If it is in an electronic format they could cut and paste. The next stage would be to put things into their own words or summarize. To help them to do this you could produce a handout with a series of questions designed to guide them towards producing a good product. By restricting the number of words or limiting the space you focus pupils' minds on the key issues. Figure 6.9 was produced by two year 9 pupils by sifting information from two articles. Another way of focusing pupils' attention is to use the idea of producing an article for a newspaper and pointing out to them that they have limited column space and a deadline (the end of the lesson).

8.3 Science dictionary

Pupils can build up their own dictionary of scientific words. This could become one of the routines followed at the end of each topic and homework exercises

THE GREENHOUSE EFFECT

The greenhouse effect is when the heat from the sun warms up the earth's atmosphere and the surface of the earth but as the earth warms up it lets off infra-red radiation. Some of this heat gets trapped by the earth's atmosphere. The 'greenhouse' gases allow more of this radiation to be trapped. There are also some natural greenhouse gases such as water vapour, nitrous oxide, carbon dioxide and methane.

WHAT CAUSES THE GREENHOUSE EFFECT?

~Growing rice
~Burning of fossil fuels such as coal and oil
~Living animals breathing
~Waste disposal

THE PROBLEMS

~Rising sea levels from the melting polar ice caps.
~Flooded lands
~Changing climate

By Beth and Rachel Evans

Figure 6.9 *A poster produced by two Y9 pupils summarizing information on the greenhouse effect*

could be based around either learning the words for a spelling test or composing a piece of writing using selected words from the list.

Practical activity 6.8

How would you deal with the following situations?

- A pupil has produced work that is beautifully presented but there are errors in the science.
- A pupil has used a graph package to draw the graph and this has joined up all the points rather than producing the line of best fit. The pupil is convinced that his graph is right because it has been produced by a computer.
- A pupil has copied large parts of his report on planets from a CD-ROM. He/she has clearly put a lot of effort into producing it but the report contains few of his/her own words.

9 USING A VIDEO

There are a large number of good videos available on a wide range of science topics and, if used well, these can make a significant contribution to pupils' learning. The first stage is for you to get to know the contents of the video and make decisions as to which parts to play to the pupils. It may be that you feel that it is necessary to play the whole tape to show how the 'story' or argument unfolds. Alternatively, you may select from the tape and fill in the 'story' yourself. You then need to think about:

- producing a worksheet related to what the pupils see;
- the number of times you would want to show key sequences;
- how you are going to break up the video into suitable sections to maintain interest.

10 THE TEACHER'S USE OF ICT

Computers can help teachers to keep on top of their administrative workload, help produce good quality teaching materials and give easy access to a wide variety of professional assistance and advice. They can also cause frustration and anger when things don't go right and can sometimes soak up vast amounts of time leading to no useful outcome. You will have to decide when it is best to use a computer or a more traditional method. You will need to develop your ICT skills throughout your teaching career as the technology improves.

10.1 Preparing worksheets

Most worksheets these days are prepared using a word processor and they are frequently put together into topic booklets. The following points are worth bearing in mind when you are writing these types of sheets:

- Is the level of the language used appropriate for the age and ability of the target pupils? (Check vocabulary and sentence length.)
- Is the layout attractive and easy to follow? (Avoid overcrowding. Use an attractive font, e.g. Comic Sans. Include clipart, but don't overdo it.)
- Include relevant diagrams and pictures where appropriate. These can be scanned, downloaded or simply photocopied and stuck in.
- Think about the purpose of the worksheet (e.g. providing pupils with information for a practical or for revision purposes, or as an exercise to help pupils to learn) and ask yourself 'Does the worksheet match my objectives?'
- What is the best form of presenting the worksheet (e.g. as a single sheet, as part of a booklet, as an electronic page)?

10.2 Using ICT to maintain records

As well as doing all the usual things like keeping electronic copies of all your worksheets, etc. (backed up, of course), you may also find it helpful to keep records of pupils' marks on a spreadsheet. This will help in working out totals for the end of term and year and converting marks into percentages. It can also be used to keep a check on certain aspects of pupils' learning, e.g. keeping track of marks allocated to specific skills. The data is useful in planning for target setting and school improvement.

10.3 Keeping up do date with developments in teaching

There are a number of websites that will help to keep you up to date with what is going on in teaching from the latest government initiatives on the DfES site to news, views and jobs on the TES site. You can find information to include in your lessons and you can even download lesson plans.

Practical activity 6.9

A science department has decided to keep records of all its pupils using a spreadsheet. A common system of end of topic tests is used for all pupils. It is therefore possible to track the progress of a pupil throughout a key stage. What do you see as the pros and cons of adopting such a system?

CONCLUSION

While there are all sorts of problems with using ICT in science, such as booking the computer room, machines not working and incompatibility of software, the potential for learning cannot be underestimated. If schools are to keep pace with developments in technology commonly found in the home and in places of work then they must make sure that pupils have easy access to up to date computers. Students on ITE courses frequently have significant expertise in using computers and you may find yourself leading the way in helping a science department to develop its ICT capability.

CHAPTER 7

Learning science through practical work

INTRODUCTION

In the UK there is a strong tradition of practical work in science lessons but over the last ten years or so, since the introduction of the National Curriculum, there has been a deepening debate over the role of practical work in promoting learning. In this chapter we will look at arguments and counter arguments for the inclusion of practical work as well as the organization and management of practical activities. By the end of this chapter you should be able to make judgements about when to include a practical task in a lesson and when to choose an alternative teaching strategy.

By the end of this chapter you should:

- understand the value of practical work in helping pupils to learn science;
- be able to set up situations that will enable pupils to carry out practical work safely and effectively;
- be able to help pupils develop their practical skills.

1 WHY DO WE USE PRACTICAL WORK IN SCIENCE LESSONS?

There are those who would argue that practical work plays an important role in the teaching of science at all levels. They would say that finding out about things through experimentation is the very essence of science and that pupils need to be taught the basics at school. They would also say that pupils enjoy practical work and that they learn by seeing things happen. Others would say that practical work doesn't always lead pupils to the correct conclusions and can cause confusion. It is expensive both in terms of time and resources and, especially when teachers feel under pressure to complete examination syllabuses, may be seen as unnecessary. Some teachers might also steer away from practical work because of the worry about safety implications and the possibility of litigation.

The National Curriculum provides teachers with some direction about practical work in the section on investigative skills and there are clearly many opportunities for practical experiences throughout each of the other programmes of study. Broadly speaking there are five areas of argument put forward for the inclusion of practical activities in science lessons. In the section below we examine each one in turn.

1.1 Motivational aspects

Many of those who have become professional scientists, or science educators, say that they were originally 'turned on' to science through a fascination of doing experiments and seeing things happen. The thrill of seeing something that is described in a textbook is difficult to describe, but any teacher who has experienced pupils shouting out 'wow, Miss that's really cool!' understands something of the effect practical work can have on pupils' motivation. Pupils in year 7 are particularly keen to do practical work, excited at the prospect of working in a 'proper' laboratory rather than the classroom-based work carried out in the primary school. It is different and exciting to work with Bunsen burners, chemicals and other 'new toys' but how long does this euphoria go on? As mentioned elsewhere (p. 157), many pupils become disenchanted with science as they work their way through key stage 3 and one possible reason for this may be that they become disillusioned with the practical work they experience. However, it is not uncommon for pupils of all ages to request practical work but we need to consider why they want to do it. Is it because they see it as an exciting and interesting activity or is it because they see it as a 'doss', an opportunity to get away from hard thinking and catch up with the latest gossip? Not all pupils, just as not all scientists, enjoy practical work and lessons must cater for their needs. There is evidence to suggest that some girls react negatively towards practical work and we, therefore, may be doing them a disservice to have a curriculum with a high practical content.

1.2 Promoting the learning of practical skills

Practical work provides pupils with the opportunity to develop a whole range of skills including the setting up of apparatus, measuring (distance, volume, time, voltage, current, etc.), predicting, observing and inferring. It could be argued that these skills are important not just in science but in many other subject areas and in life at home and, later on, in work. If this is true, practical science is making a valuable contribution to the development of skills that will be of value to individuals for the rest of their lives. However, the situation may not be as simple as this. There is some evidence to show that the skills learnt in one subject may not be transferable to another. Learning at one level tends to be compartmentalized and it may be a struggle for an individual to apply skills learnt in one subject to a completely different situation.

1.3 Promoting logical thinking

There are a number of ways that practical work can help pupils develop logical thinking. In carrying out a practical there must be a set sequence setting up the equipment, following the experimental procedure and taking the measurements. In the design of an investigation, pupils have to consider the variables and make decisions on which to vary, which to keep constant and which to measure. In observing what goes on in a practical they need to apply logic and scientific knowledge to make sense of the results. But how much freedom does the teacher give the pupils to use logic? For all sorts of reasons teachers tend to do a lot of the thinking for pupils and guide them into doing the right thing rather than let them make their own mistakes.

1.4 Improving pupils' understanding

Many school practicals clearly illustrate what is in the textbook or syllabus and, as such, help the pupils to visualize and remember the situation. Teachers often refer back to practical events and use them as a memory jogger and a landmark in pupils' learning: 'Do you remember when we did . . . well what did it tell us about . . . now what do you think would happen if . . . why do you think that?' The teacher's explanation and the class discussion that goes along with the practical both play a pivotal role in helping pupils to understand. But not all practicals help pupils to understand. There are those that cause confusion because they are so complicated that the meaning of the experiment is lost in the 'noise' of the procedure used to carry it out. There are simple experiments when we as teachers can clearly see the conclusion that follows from the results but we need to bear in mind that pupils may find it difficult to make the necessary logical connections. Then there are those experiments that 'don't work' or don't give the 'right' answer. Pupils are often unimpressed with the teacher's explanation of why things have gone wrong and it only takes one or two of these events for pupils to be convinced that science doesn't work.

1.5 Providing opportunities for group discussion and the development of team skills

In most instances pupils carry out practical work in groups, not just because there isn't enough apparatus to go round, but because it provides an opportunity for pupils to work together on a science task and to learn from each other. Decisions need to be made within the group as to who does what and when, so that all members of the team have the opportunity to practice skills and take responsibility. In some cases the teacher will have planned a series of questions for pupils to discuss or for individuals to think about while the practical is proceeding. Discussion can take place while pupils are waiting for something to happen or immediately after the practical has finished. The questions could be centred around asking pupils to consider why they are following a particular procedure or to provide an explanation of their results in terms of what they have learnt so far. If left to their own devices the conversations around the apparatus are likely to focus on inconsequential matters. If teamwork is not encouraged it is likely that the responsibility for the whole practical falls on the shoulders of one individual while the other two members of the group get on with something else or just chat.

At this stage it could be said that practical work has the potential to help pupils to learn science but a lot depends on the activity and how the teacher presents and manages the work and the quality of the class discussion that follows.

You could consider the value of a practical exercise by asking yourself the following questions:

- Have the pupils learnt new skills and/or knowledge?
- Have they been able to engage with others about their experiment?
- Have they found the exercise interesting?
- Have they been intellectually challenged by the activity?
- Has pupils' curiosity been aroused?

Practical activity 7.1

Review the practical activities you have carried out during a set period of time, e.g. one or two weeks. Consider the following:

- To what extent have these experiments motivated the pupils?
  (Look for things such as pupil enjoyment, pupil involvement. Has the experiment aroused curiosity, etc.?)
- What have the pupils learnt by doing the experiments?
  (Have the experiments resulted in clear learning outcomes? Do the pupils refer to the results of the experiment in class discussion?)
- Could the same learning be achieved by any other means?
  (If there are other ways of achieving the same goals you need to consider the advantages and disadvantages of each method.)

2 DIFFERENT SORTS OF PRACTICAL WORK

'Are we doin' a 'speriment today Miss?'

While the term 'experiment' is often used for the activities carried out in science lessons, frequently what goes on bears no resemblance to the procedures used in a research laboratory. School experiments tend, on the whole, to be a repetition of tried and tested situations and do not find out something new or test hypotheses. The nearest we have to 'real' experiments are the investigations of the NC, but before we look at that we will consider how best to categorize all the other different types of practical work used in schools. These will generally fall into one of the two following headings:

1. *Basic practical skills*
   This includes activities such as enabling pupils to use standard laboratory equipment and carry out simple practical routines. Some of these skills will be taught in year 7 (e.g. how to light a Bunsen burner), but the majority will be taught when the task requires them. It is worth bearing in mind that pupils may use these skills infrequently and will need reminding of the correct way of carrying out techniques from time to time. For example, they may learn early about how to measure volumes accurately by having an eye level with the meniscus but may need reminding of the correct technique from time to time to avoid the development of bad habits.

Practical activity 7.2

If pupils are not using particular techniques on a regular basis they tend to forget how to do them correctly.

Make a point of checking on pupils' practical skills from time to time. For example, you could warn the pupils that during the next two weeks you are going to be testing them on practical skills. Carry this out and then give feedback on their performance.

2. *Illustrating a theory or concept*

A lot of school practical work falls under this heading. Teachers use practicals in this way to help pupils understand, or remember, a particular phenomenon. The principle is one of 'seeing is believing' and many pupils benefit from linking these observations to the theory they have learnt in another part of the lesson.

Looking at any of the textbooks produced for key stage 3 science will show that the authors, at least, consider that practical work should form a major part of the curriculum. Naturally, these tasks are presented as a series of instructions to follow – how else would the pupil know what to do? But, as teachers, we need to consider the messages that repeated use of this approach might be giving to our pupils. For example, are we saying that science is all about following tried and tested routines to give us the right answer? To be fair, the textbooks try to get away from the image that science simply involves following recipes by adding questions to get the pupils to think about what they are doing and why they are doing it.

Practical activity 7.3

Examine the scheme of work for one of the topics you are teaching and carry out an audit of the practical work used, classifying it under one of the following headings:

- Learning basic practical skills
- Illustrating a theory or concept
- Open investigative work (see Figure 7.2)
- Closed investigative work.

Examine a key stage 3 textbook and consider how it classifies the different types of practical work. How does their classification match with the one above?

In general, how are the practical activities presented to pupils? Take one or two examples and consider what are the opportunities for pupils to think scientifically and to be challenged intellectually.

3 | PLANNING FOR PRACTICAL WORK

There are plenty of opportunities for things to go wrong during a practical so you must manage the situation carefully. The first step is ordering the equipment from the technician. Your request needs to be clear in all respects and should include details of the time, date and room you will be using. It is worthwhile talking through the experiment with the technician as he or she has probably seen the practical carried out many times before and knows where the problems lie. You should carry out the practical using the equipment the pupils are going to use to satisfy yourself that everything will go to plan on the day. It may come as a surprise to you that what looks like a very simple practical can have hidden problems. The next step is to consider how you, or the technician, are going to lay out the equipment so that it can be collected by the pupils safely and with the minimum of fuss. An orderly, table by table or row by row, approach should eliminate any squabbling over the 'best kit' and subsequent breakages. Through-out the activity you need to be vigilant to ensure that the pupils are working safely and be prepared to deal with any problems quickly. If an accident occurs you must first make sure that the pupils are ok and that the situation is rendered safe before trying to determine if something simply went wrong or if the pupils were to blame. You need to watch very carefully what the pupils are doing and make judgements about how long it will take them to finish the task. Some pupils are skilled at spinning out the time to do a practical if they know that they will have to do something less exciting, such as writing, as soon as the practical is over. You will need to make a clear decision about when to stop the practical and tell this to the pupils. The next dilemma you are faced with is whether or not to collect the apparatus as soon as the practical is over or to leave it until nearer the end of the lesson. Collecting it immediately after the practical has the advantage of clearing the desks ready for the next activity but may have the drawback that pupils think they have finished for the day and pack away their books as well as the apparatus. This problem can be overcome by warning the pupils about what is going to happen next (an advanced organizer). If the apparatus is left on the desks it is possible that pupils will fiddle with it and not concentrate on the concluding parts of the lesson. It is a good idea to have the apparatus placed out of reach of the pupils in a suitable place and in an appropriate condition for the technician to clear away. Frequently technicians have to run around from lab to lab sorting things out at the change of lesson time and they appreciate anything you can do to make their job easier.

4 | SAFETY ISSUES

Thankfully, major accidents in the laboratory are relatively rare. However, it is incumbent upon teachers to make sure that pupils and themselves work in a safe environment. You can reduce the risk of having an accident by following a few simple rules:

- When planning your lesson, think carefully about when things could possibly go wrong.
- Try out all practical activities in advance of the lesson and identify the possible risks.
- Make sure that both you and your pupils work in a clutter free environment.
- Train your pupils to think about safety (useful information sheets for pupils are avalable from CLEAPSS, 2000a).
- Always be vigilant and be prepared to intervene when it looks like things are going wrong or when pupils start to misbehave.

You need to be particularly careful about the wearing of eye protection. Safety glasses or goggles need to be worn whenever:

- liquids are being used (with the possible exception of water at room temperature);
- something is being heated;
- there is a risk of objects flying through the air (e.g. stretched wires breaking).

It should go without saying that the glasses need to be worn correctly but some pupils find it amusing to wear them on various parts of their head other than over their eyes. Some dislike goggles, either because they don't find them comfortable or because they spoil their hair style. You need to be very insistent and give reminders, both verbally and written on the board and set a good example by wearing them yourself.

There are plenty of publications giving guidance on health and safety issues. In particular you will find it helpful to consult:

- the school's (and/or science department's) health and safety policy;
- Topics in Safety (ASE, 2001)
- Safeguards in the School Laboratory (ASE, 1996)
- Safety in Science Education (DfEE, 1996)
- Hazcards (a set of cards listing the hazards associated with common chemicals used in schools) (CLEAPSS, 2000b)

Figure 7.1 points out some of the common safety things that you need to be aware of when carrying out practical work. The most common accidents are pupils getting chemicals in their eyes or on other parts of their bodies.

Practical activity 7.3

Consider how you are going to get your pupils to work safely in the laboratory.

- How will you make sure that they know the safety rules in year 7?
- How will you make sure that all the pupils are wearing safety glasses during a practical? What will you do to pupils who won't wear them?
- What will you do if a pupil spills some acid on the bench?
- What will you do if pupils misbehave during a practical activity?

Situation	What you need to consider
Using a Bunsen burner	• Be aware that pupils can't see a blue flame in a light room. • Make sure that the flame goes nowhere near flammable solvents. Use a water bath to heat ethanol, etc. • Pupils forget that it takes time for a tripod and gauze to cool down.
Fires	• You should know how to switch off the gas at the mains. • You should know how to put out small fires without causing too much fuss (you need to be aware that sometimes when the teacher over-reacts to a situation the pupils want a repeat performance. Don't use a carbon dioxide fire extinguisher when a damp cloth will do). • You should know how to get your pupils out of the lab quickly and safely.
Using acids and bases	• Safety glasses/goggles are essential. Alkalis, as well as acids, can cause serious damage to eyes. • Make sure pupils replace stoppers on the bottles to reduce spills. • Be aware that some pupils may try to squirt liquids at each other if teat pipettes are used. • Wash any parts of the body that are contaminated with plenty of water.
Chemical reactions	• Safety glasses/goggles are essential. • Make sure that you are aware of the hazards involved. Use safe amounts and carry out all the necessary safety procedures. • Consider safe ways of distributing the materials. • Make sure you know how to dispose of the waste at the end of the practical. • Be aware that some chemicals can permanently change the colour of some clothes.
Glassware	• You should know what to do about broken glass to avoid pupils being injured. • Get the pupil to clean any cut and take appropriate action dependant on the size of the cut.
Pressure experiments	• When using a model steam engine make sure that the pressure release valve operates freely. • Make sure that everyone is protected when there is a possibility of implosion or explosion (e.g. tape around the vessel, safety screen, safety glasses).

Continued

Situation	What you need to consider
Electrical experiments	• Make sure that there is no risk of pupils electrocuting themselves. • Only use equipment that has been tested and is electrically safe.
Biological samples	• Only use animals or parts of animals from approved sources, except things like worms and woodlice. • Do not use human body fluids, e.g. saliva, blood.
Always carry out the experiment prior to the lesson **Think about where things could go wrong** **Carry out a risk assessment when appropriate**	

Figure 7.1 *Some points worthy of consideration when carrying out practical work*

5   ORGANIZING THE PRACTICAL ACTIVITY

Your choice of how to organize the practical activity will depend on the amount of apparatus available, the safety of the experiment and the degree to which you want pupils to work together. There are three common arrangements:

- groups of pupils, or an individual, working on one experiment;
- pupils following a circus of small practical tasks;
- teacher demonstration.

5.1   Group practical

The most common approach to practical work is to ask two or three pupils to work together on a task. This usually works well and everyone benefits as:

- responsibilities are shared;
- members of the group are not distracted by social 'chit chat', etc.;
- everyone has a copy of the results.

5.2   Circus of tasks

You would set up a circus of activities around the laboratory when you want pupils to experience a variety of tasks. A series of mini tasks arranged in this sort of way can prompt a great deal of thinking, as pupils are presented with something a little bit different at each station of the circus. One common example of using a circus approach is in the teaching of energy when pupils need to study a range of energy transfers. Each of the activities takes only a few minutes to do practically, including thinking and writing time. Not all stations of the circus need involve a practical task. There are a number of other things pupils can do such as a reading and writing exercise or working on a computer. In order to run the circus efficiently teachers need to allocate a fixed period of time after which the pupils move on to the next station. This may require additional writing tasks being set where the practical can be completed quickly. The instructions at each station will need to be written clearly (preferably on laminated card for protection) to avoid you having to rush around explaining what to do. When all the pupils have completed all the activities it is a good idea to check what they have found out and how they have benefited from the experiences by asking the following types of questions:

- What happened at station X? (Get another group to confirm.) Is that what you saw happening?
- What does that tell us about . . .?
- Why do you think it did that?
- If I were to change the . . . for a . . ., what do you think would happen?
- Can you explain that in terms of what we did last lesson?

Further ideas about the use of circuses is given in *Teaching Science* Frost *et al.*, 1995).

5.3 Demonstrations

Demonstrations are usually done when the equipment is very expensive or when the practical activity is too dangerous, difficult or time-consuming to be done by all the pupils. There is an art to demonstrating, it is not simply like carrying out your own experiment in front of the class. You need to involve the class as much as possible in the practical by having the apparatus 'facing' towards the class and by maintaining a dialogue with the pupils about what is happening. There are a number of things you need to bear in mind when carrying out a demonstration:

- *The size and position of the apparatus* – ensure that pupils can see what is going on by choosing apparatus that is reasonably large and by suitable positioning of the demonstration. You also need to check that the appropriate services (water, gas, and electricity) are near to hand.
- *The position of the pupils during the demonstration* – all pupils must be comfortable and be able to see. The best arrangement is for pupils to sit on their stools in a semicircle around the demonstration.
- *Safety* – if there is a risk of an explosion or implosion pupils must be protected from the apparatus by a safety screen and both you and the pupils should wear eye protection. Some appalling accidents have occurred when these safety precautions have not been taken.
- *Explanations and questions* – bearing in mind that it is difficult to do two things at once you need to plan out what you are going to say to the pupils during the demonstration and what questions you are going to ask them. Try to avoid long periods where you are involved with the apparatus and the pupils are left to watch in silence (hopefully!).

6 PROMOTING PUPILS' THINKING

One of your aims should be to lift the practical activity from one where pupils are simply 'playing' with the apparatus or following a recipe to one where pupils are intellectually involved with what they are doing. A teacher can alter the intellectual demand of any practical activity by the way she/he presents the practical and the questions posed during the activity. You can ask the pupils to try to explain what is happening or you can ask a number of 'why' questions, such as:

- Why did I ask you to set up the apparatus in this way?
- Why did we do things in this sequence rather than the other way around?
- Why did you see bubbles forming? What do you think they were?
- Why did that happen? Can you explain it in terms of particles?
- Why did you get that result rather than the one we were expecting?

7 INVESTIGATIONS

Investigations are about finding out things and, as such, there are a whole range of different types of activities that can come under the heading of 'investigations'. It is useful to be able to categorize them in order to help with the planning of the curriculum to ensure that pupils have a range of worthwhile experiences. Categorizing is also helpful when we come to consider the cognitive and practical demands we are making on the pupils. Reading the section in the National Curriculum entitled Investigative Skills which will be found in the Scientific Enquiry programme of study will give you an initial idea of what is involved. The first strand to Investigative Skills requires that pupils to be taught how to plan investigations. We cannot assume that pupils will simply pick up the knowledge about how to plan an investigation from their previous experiences of practical work. For example, they may have difficulty in distinguishing between the important and the trivial, they are frequently unsure about the range of data to collect and may not know which is the more appropriate type of apparatus to use. At various stages of pupils' development it is important, therefore, to have teacher-directed investigations where planning skills are taught. Investigations are best done towards the end of a topic to give pupils the opportunity to apply some of the knowledge gained in the previous weeks. As with any other type of practical work, investigations need to be carried out in advance by the teacher. You may have thought things through carefully beforehand but simple things can always catch you out and pupils can become very demotivated if they spend a long time working on a project and get no usable results.

There are a number of ways that the teacher can present an investigation or prompt pupils to suggest an investigation and these are summarized in Figure 7.2. From time to time investigations will be teacher-directed in order to help pupils develop new skills, but as pupils become more proficient they will need to

Teacher-directed Pupils learn about the craft of experimental design	**Pupil-planned** Requires pupils to apply prior knowledge to a new situation
Open investigations There are many ways of doing the investigation and many acceptable solutions to the problem	**Closed investigations** There is only one 'correct' answer to the investigation and one way of achieving it
Pupil-initiated As part of their on-going work pupils generate ideas that can be investigated	**Teacher-initiated** The teacher directs pupils to situations that can be investigated

Figure 7.2 *Ways of presenting an investigation*

be given greater responsibility for developing their own plans. Investigations are sometimes described as open or closed. A closed investigation will have only one solution and generally only have one way of achieving it whereas an open investigation will have many solutions and many ways of carrying out the experiment. Jones *et al.* (1992) have indicted that there are many potential learning opportunities with open-ended work and, while it may be more time consuming than other practical activities, it can have significant benefits for pupils' learning. Because teachers need to progress through the curriculum at a steady pace and prepare pupils for examinations the majority of investigations used at present are teacher-initiated. However, by carefully planned discussion, or good luck, it is sometimes possible for teachers to move the class discussion round to such a point that pupils think they have generated the idea for the investigation.

7.1 Range of investigations

Watson *et al.* (1999) have classified the investigations carried out in schools into six broad types:

1. *Classifying and identifying*
   - Examples – developing a key to classify rocks/animals/plants, identification of patterns of behaviour.
   - Possible framing – what have these animals got in common and in what ways are they different? What happens when metal carbonates react with acid?

2. *Fair testing*
   - Examples – experiments involving the determination of rate of reaction, cooling can investigations, resistance of a wire investigations.
   - Possible framing – what are the factors that affect the rate at which marble chips react with hydrochloric acid? Which insulator is the best? What factors affect the electrical resistance of a wire?

3. *Pattern seeking*
   - Examples – investigations where variables cannot be easily controlled such as fieldwork and surveys.
   - Possible framing – what plants grow near a hedge? Where do we find the most snails in the garden? Which countries use the most oil and what do they use it for?

4. *Investigating models*
   - Examples – modelling heat loss by animals or buildings, modelling lava flow, model of predator–prey relationship.
   - Possible framing – what is the best way of preventing heat loss? What is the relationship between the numbers of foxes and the number of rabbits?

5. *Exploring*
   - Examples – rust formation over time (exploring the amount of rust formed under different conditions), the shape of the moon over time.
   - Possible framing – what are the best conditions for rust formation? What might this tell us about the reactions that take place when rust is formed?

6. *Making things or developing systems*
   - Examples – making a water purification system from different sizes of granular material, making a rain meter.
   - Possible framing – design a system to purify a sample of pond water. Design a device that could be used to let you know when to bring the washing in from the line.

7.2 Teaching about investigations

Pupils who have carried out a series of CASE activities (see p. 31) should have a good understanding about variables and fair testing and have a firm foundation on which to build their investigation work.

Planning an investigation can be quite a difficult task for many pupils. It may be that this is the only time they are asked to prepare a significant piece of writing about science and they may find the phrasing and vocabulary difficult. This is in addition to having to cope with difficult science concepts and procedures. It is, therefore, advisable to guide pupils through the planning by asking them a series of questions that will lead them in the right direction. Figure 7.3 lists a series of questions that could be given to pupils attempting a fair testing type of investigation.

Once pupils start to carry out their investigations, and this can take three to four hours at key stage 4, the teacher adopts the role of advisor and guide. As pupils can feel very insecure as they work their way through the investigation they will need:

- help with the experimental techniques;
- reminding of the science required for the investigation;
- help with finding other sources of information;
- guidance about which data to record and when to record it (including a reminder not to write results on scraps of paper);
- help with thinking about the validity of their results;
- guidance on how to present their results and, where appropriate, depict the

Section/question on planning sheet	Comment
Title of investigation	This should try to describe as accurately as possible what the investigation is trying to find out. It should help to focus the pupils' minds on the objectives of the investigation.
What are you going to find out?	Give the pupils further opportunity to clarify what is being investigated by constructing statements that can be clearly translated into an experimental procedure.
What do you think will happen?	The pupils can make a prediction if appropriate.
Why do you think this will happen?	The pupils need to be prompted to consider what aspects of learnt science can be brought to bear on this problem.
What are the variables?	A class or group brainstorming activity is an effective way of coming up with a list of variables. It may then be necessary to eliminate some as insignificant or irrelevant.
What will you change in your investigation?	This is an opportunity to reinforce that in order to be 'fair' only one thing can be changed at a time.
What will you measure/observe?	The pupils need to consider which type of data is going to be more meaningful and, at GCSE level in particular, what is likely to result in higher marks.
What will you keep constant?	The pupils need to consider how all the other variables can be kept constant.
How many measurements will you take?	When possible, pupils should take repeat readings to check for consistency of results and improve the reliability of their data.
What apparatus/instruments will you use to make your measurements?	The pupils need to consider the scale of the experiment and the types of measuring instruments that are going to lead to the most accurate results.
How will you make sure that you carry out the investigation safely?	The pupils need to take some responsibility for the safety of the investigation. It may be advisable for them to consult the CLEAPSS Student Safety Sheets.

Figure 7.3 *Guidance for pupils in planning an investigation*

Independent variable	Dependent variable	Control variable	Derived variable
The fact that the investigator changes systematically	The fact that the investigator measures	The factors that the investigator keeps constant during the investigation	Calculated from the results of the experiment
The alcohol, i.e. CH_3OH C_2H_5OH C_3H_7OH C_4H_9OH	Temperature rise of water	• Volume of the water • Distance of the flame from the water • Mass (or volume) of the alcohol	Heat transferred (kJ) = mass of water (kg) × temperature rise (°C) × 4.2

Figure 7.4 *Types of variables in an investigation of the heat evolved by buring different fuels. Suitable fuels are methanol, ethanol, propan-l-ol, butan-l-ol. The burning fuel raises the temperature of a volume of water. Heat loss should be kept to a minimum and it is assumed that the heat given off in combustion equals the heat absorbed by the water*

    information graphically (see Goldsworthy *et al.*, 1999, for useful guidance on graph work);

- help in matching their conclusions to the results obtained and in making realistic decisions as to how their experiment could have been improved.

For some pupils this sort of help will always be needed but, hopefully, many pupils will be able to make progress on their own or with minimum support.

    It is important to spend some class discussion time at the end of the investigation drawing together what has been learnt from the experience and how to apply this new learning to the next investigation.

    If pupils have carried out a particularly successful investigation they may consider submitting it to the Investigations website at *www.sci-journal.org/index.html*. This also serves as a useful list of ideas for teachers.

7.3 Types of variables

Pupils need to learn the language of investigations, particularly the names given to the different sorts of variables used in fair testing investigations. All variables fall into one of the following groups:

- categoric – a non-numeric variable, e.g. colour, nature of material, shape;
- discrete – a variable that can only have whole number values, e.g. numbers of layers, number of turns of a wire, number of tablets;
- continuous – a variable that can have any numeric value, e.g. distance, volume, time, temperature, voltage.

These types of variables are illustrated in Figure 7.4 for the investigation into the combustion of the homologous series of alcohols.

In a fair testing investigation the pupil makes a decision as to which variables to keep constant (the control variables) and which one to change (the independent variable). The thing that the pupil measures is called the dependent variable. An example of these different types of variables is shown in Figure 7.5 for a KS4 investigation. The temperature rise produced by the burning alcohol can be converted, using a standard formula, into an enthalpy of combustion. When a calculation of this nature is done the resulting values are called derived variables.

7.4 Progression in practical abilities

A great deal of emphasis is placed on developing pupils' investigative skills in the primary school but it appears that many secondary schools fail to build on this experience by teaching a KS3 curriculum that is almost devoid of investigations, as illustrated in the following comment from an Ofsted report.

> Experimental and investigative science often receives little explicit attention during Y7 and Y8. Teachers feel under pressure to cover content and see investigative work as time-consuming and less relevant to measurable performance.
>
> (Ofsted, 2000)

Another problem that sometimes occurs is the repetition of investigations as pupils progress through school, for example Watson *et al*. (1999) report on their research which shows that some investigations carried out at KS2 (dissolving sugar in water, heat loss from insulated cans) are repeated at KS3.

These sorts of situations do not portray the right sort of image of science to pupils, as well as having a negative effect on their learning. You need to help pupils develop their practical abilities by presenting them with new and challenging situations. In planning practical work for pupils over a long period of time you should look for activities that would enable them to improve their:

- manipulative and observational skills;
- ability to interpret the results of experiments from their growing knowledge of science;
- appreciation of the value of practical work as part of scientific endeavour;
- ability to tackle practical problems;
- ability to plan and carry out investigative work.

Practical activity 7.4

Select three investigations that pupils are asked to do, one from year 7, one from year 9 and one from year 11. Consider the cognitive and practical demands made on the pupils at each age and identify aspects of progression.

7.5 Investigations for GCSE examinations

At key stage 4 teachers clearly have at the back of their minds the GCSE course work assessment requirements and it is likely that the activities presented to

Investigation	What factors affect the rate of photosynthesis (using Elodea in water)?	What factors affect the electrical resistance of a length of wire?	What is the effect of caffeine on the heartbeat?	Investigating the distribution and abundance of invertebrates in a pond	What affects the rate of reaction between magnesium and hydrochloric acid?
Variables	• Temperature • Light intensity • Carbon dioxide concentration • Amount of Elodea	• Length of the wire • Cross-sectional area of the wire • Material the wire is made from • The temperature of the wire	• Mass of instant coffee • Volume of coffee drunk • Temperature of coffee and room • Amount of exercise done prior to drinking the coffee	• Sampling site in the pond • Temperature of the water • Surrounding vegetation • Season • Weather over preceding period	• Mass of magnesium • Type of magnesium (lumps, powder, ribbon, etc.) • Concentration of acid • Temperature of acid

Figure 7.5 *The range of variables in a number of different investigations*

pupils will be designed in such a way as to ensure that they have the maximum opportunity for gaining high marks. Not unnaturally many teachers will resort to tried and tested methods and use only a limited range of investigations. With this sort of approach the intellectual challenge for pupils falls as they are asked to do little more than follow a set routine.

Teachers need to consider the demand of the task in terms of the associated scientific knowledge, manipulation, precision and accuracy and complexity. The simple tasks will not enable pupils to gain the higher marks in each of the skill areas. Pruden (1999) provides teachers with a useful resource identifying a number of investigations suitable for GCSE and indicates which ones offer the best opportunities for obtaining high marks in the four skill areas. GCSE examination boards also provide teachers with samples of marked coursework and it is worthwhile checking these very carefully to identify what is required for full marks.

If pupils are given the task of planning an open-ended investigation it is important that the teacher checks that the pupils has considered all the necessary safety precautions before he/she carries out the experiment.

CONCLUSION

Part of the 'magic' and appeal of science is about finding things out for yourself. It is about being inquisitive and venturing into the unknown. The chemistry Nobel Laureate, Max Perutz puts it very eloquently:

> Science has changed the world, but the scientists who changed it rarely foresaw the revolutions to which their research would lead. Like children out on a treasure hunt, scientists don't know what they will find.
>
> (Perutz, 1998, p. x)

Practical work can play an enormous role in helping to illustrate to pupils how scientists think and work. But in order to do this, the tasks need to be properly framed and linked to useful learning outcomes. To ask pupils to follow a series of instructions and not require them to question what they are doing is simply a waste of time.

CHAPTER 8

Using assessment effectively

INTRODUCTION

The word 'assessment' can conjure up a lot of frightening images for the person being assessed. There is the possibility of failure or not doing quite as well as your friends. There are still problems when you become a teacher such as having to deal with mountains of books to mark and the tedious task of chasing up pupils who haven't handed their work in on time. However, assessment plays a vital role in education and in this chapter you will find out about how it can be carried out efficiently, with as much enjoyment and as little teacher stress as possible.

The government and the media, particularly newspapers, have given a great deal of emphasis to assessment data in recent years. The publishing of examination results has been used as part of the strategy to raise standards and to compare schools in similar catchment areas. There is a danger that the emphasis on results is becoming disproportionate to all the other things that schools achieve. It is worth bearing in mind the comment made by Peter Johnson, Head of Millfield, quoted in *The Times Educational Supplement* (17 November 2000):

> People in positions of influence seem to have forgotten that the best things in education are often those that cannot be measured.

Education is about helping young people to understand themselves and relate positively to others. It is about generating an interest in learning and helping them to become good citizens. All of which is very difficult to quantify.

By the end of this chapter you should:

- understand the principles of assessment;
- understand how to use assessment to help pupils to learn;
- know how to set tests and mark books;
- understand the organization of external examinations;
- know how practical work is assessed in external examinations.

1 THE PURPOSE OF ASSESSMENT

Assessment has got a reputation of being a very exact discipline (and to a certain extent it is worthy of this status) but once you begin to delve deeper you will see that it is far more than telling a pupil that he or she is right or wrong. Assessment also involves the whole process of helping pupils and teachers to improve what they are doing. It requires clarity in terms of what we want the pupils to learn all the way from examination syllabuses through to the objectives for individual lessons. It is about the development of skills and the presentation of work as well as the accumulation of knowledge. At different times in a school year assessment should fulfil each of four main aims:

- It should assist and support pupils in the learning of science *(it should be formative)*.
- It should assist in identifying where pupils are going wrong in their learning and what can be done about it *(it should be diagnostic)*.
- It should assist science teachers in evaluating their own performance, the effectiveness of the department and of the school in promoting learning *(it should be evaluative)*.
- It should provide information (for pupils, parents, employers, etc.) about progress at key end points in the learning, e.g. end of topic, end of year, GCSE examinations *(it should be summative)*.

Over the years research has shown that improving learning through assessment depends on five, deceptively simple key factors:

- the provision of effective feedback to pupils;
- the active involvement of pupils in their own learning;
- adjusting teaching to take account of the results of assessment;
- a recognition of the profound influence assessment has on the motivation and self-esteem of pupils, both of which are crucial influences on learning;
- the need for pupils to assess themselves and understand how to improve.

(Assessment Reform Group, 1999, p. 4)

In the sections that follow you will see how these factors are put into practice by teachers.

2 | PRINCIPLES OF ASSESSMENT

If you were given the task of devising an assessment system from scratch what underlying principles would you apply? You might go for a system that is purely based on marks out of ten using the argument that it is easy to handle and readily gives you a percentage at the end of term. Or you may opt for a system based on grades A, B, C, etc., with each letter having a specific meaning, on the basis that some types of work don't lend themselves to a numerical mark. Or you may go for some system that involves a combination of marks and grades. There are positive features and drawbacks with whatever system you choose but, when making the decision, it is worth bearing in mind a few guiding principles. Any assessment system should be:

- *readily understood by pupils and teachers* – you might also include parents in the list. Does the scheme show how much progress individuals are making and what they need to do to improve? What exactly does 7/10 or C mean?
- *reliable and valid* – if you have two different assessment strategies to test pupils' understanding of a concept you would have to make a judgement about the reliability of each. Are both methods comparable or equally reliable

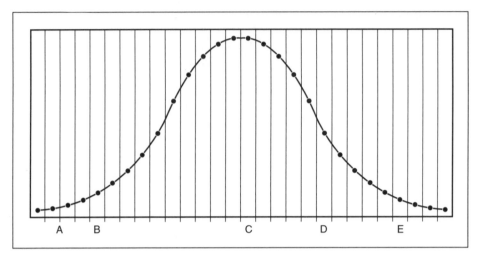

Figure 8.1 *Normal distribution of marks in an examination linked to grades*

measures of what you want to test? Does a written question on practical work test practical skills? A valid assessment is one that tests what it sets out to test;

- *positive* – it must allow pupils to demonstrate what they know and can do rather than ask them questions that they have no hope of answering. This principle is used in the tiered system of examinations at the end of KS3 and GCSE.

- *compatible with external examination requirements* – it is useful to have a system that is similar to the key features of the national tests at KS3 and the GCSE. For example investigative work could be marked on a very similar basis to that required for GCSE exams throughout the school.

- *easy to use* – assessment systems that are made up of many subdivisions are destined to fail as people become confused or forget to fill in some of the categories.

3 | NORM AND CRITERION REFERENCING

If you were to set a test to a sample of the population you would expect the results to lie on a normal distribution. A few people would get very high marks and a few very low with the vast amount lying in the bulge somewhere between. External examinations used to be graded using this sort of system. The distribution of percentage marks would be recorded and the resultant graphical representation of the data would approximate to a normal distribution (Figure 8.1, where the x-axis is number of examination candidates and the y-axis is percentage marks, starting with 100 per cent on the left-hand side). Vertical lines would be drawn on the graph representing the grade boundaries for A, B, C, D, etc. You can see from the graph that these would not be evenly distributed, as there are only a few A but a large number of C grades. It didn't matter if the examination was slightly harder or easier each year because all that you had to do was to move the vertical line to the left or to the right to make sure that roughly the same percentage of pupils were awarded each grade. The assumption was made that the population of pupils taking the examination each year had roughly the same intellectual spread.

With a criterion-referenced examination system there are a series of criteria that pupils must meet if they are to be awarded a particular grade. So, in theory, it is possible for every member of the population to meet the criteria for an A grade. Clearly this couldn't happen under a norm-based system. The GCSE examination is now run on a modified criterion-based system making it possible for schools to increase the number of pupils getting 5 A*–C passes.

A strict criterion-based system would involve ticking off each of the criteria linked to a particular grade. If all the boxes weren't ticked then that pupil could not be awarded the grade. You may find some haggard-looking teachers who remember such a system in the early days of the NC. In the present NC you will find level descriptions for each of the levels. These are more like pen portraits of what you would expect of a pupil who had attained a particular level. There is no requirement that a pupil should satisfy each of the statements in the description – so long as she/he fits the general picture it can be said that the level has been reached.

4   METHODS OF ASSESSMENT

Teachers use a variety of methods for assessing their pupils. There are the usual methods such as marking their books and tests and the less formal methods involving the day to day interactions with pupils. You can ask pupils' questions, get them to explain things or talk to each other in small groups. Simply listening to what pupils say can give you an enormous insight into their level of understanding. In order to get a valid picture of a pupil's ability in science you need to use a range of different assessment techniques.

One of your aims for assessment may be that, as far as possible, it should be a positive experience for each pupil. Pupils like to know that they have achieved something in their science lessons. It helps them to feel good about themselves and provides them with an incentive to go on learning the subject.

Practical activity 8.1

Make sure that you are familiar with the assessment policy of your department and are clear about the procedures for marking work and keeping records.

- How does the system ensure that pupils get regular feedback on their progress?
- How does the system provide you with information for reporting to parents in terms of ability to communicate science, numerical and graphical skills, practical skills, understanding of science, etc.?
- How does the system aim to improve learning and raise standards?

5 | MARKING PUPILS' WRITTEN WORK

You will have to accept that marking is going to take up a lot of time and make judgements about which work needs detailed marking and which work can be marked fairly superficially. You will find it beneficial to collect books in on a regular basis to ensure that pupils get into a routine and to make sure that you don't develop an enormous backlog of work to mark.

When marking a piece of written work the teacher has to consider what to give credit for and what needs to be corrected. If the purpose of the piece of writing is to help pupils develop their understanding of science then it may be counterproductive to correct every wrong spelling and grammar mistake. However, you need to bear in mind that a small percentage of marks at GCSE will be awarded for correct spelling, punctuation and grammar. It would therefore be advisable to comment separately on pupils' correct use of science and English.

You should try to be as helpful as possible with the comments you write on pupils' books. It is of little use writing things such as *'could do better'* or *'you need to try harder'* as they give no indication as to where the pupils should be placing their effort. It is much more helpful to point out where pupils have gone wrong and give them a clear indication as to what they should do to improve. If you find that you are saying the same thing over and over again then you need to ask yourself why the pupil isn't making any progress. It may be the case that you want the pupil to improve the presentation of his/her work but the pupil doesn't know what to do to achieve this, so you need to go into detail explaining about use of a ruler, layout of the page, etc.

You can use the idea of marking as an interesting learning task for pupils. You can supply them with a piece of work either of your own composition or taken from a past pupil, suitably modified so the person cannot be identified, and ask pupils to mark it. If you choose work where the scientific explanations are not quite right you may find that pupils will say at first that there is nothing wrong with it. You can then ask them to look more closely. This sort of activity helps to improve pupils' writing precision and possibly eliminate some misconceptions.

Practical activity 8.2

Take a piece of work completed by pupils towards the end of a topic you have taught in Year 9. This could be the end of topic test, a homework or the write up of an investigation. Using the NC level descriptions, assign a level to the work for all the pupils in the class and justify your decisions by writing a few comments on each piece of work.

With your mentor:

- Discuss your reasons for allocating each level.
- Discuss the pros and cons of 'levelling' pieces of work throughout the key stage.
- How would you help a pupil to make progress to a higher level?

Topic / Assessment objectives	Properties of metals	Reaction with oxygen	Corrosion of metals	Getting metals from rocks	Recycling metals
Knowledge and understanding	1, 6, 7	2, 10	2, 12	5, 6, 11	12a
Application of knowledge	9	4	3		
Analysis and evaluation	7			8	12b

Figure 8.2 *Analysing a twelve question test on metals in terms of coverage of topics and assessment objectives*

6 | SETTING TESTS

Many KS3 published science schemes have sample tests in the Teachers' Guides. Teachers also have access to large numbers of past questions, e.g. KS3 tests, GCSE and A-level exam papers, as well as published questions. In putting these together or in devising your own questions for a test it is worth bearing in mind a few basic principles.

- Make sure that the questions relate to the present syllabus or NC.
- Check that the level of questions is appropriate for all the pupils. You want all pupils to achieve some success. This may involve using tiered question papers or questions of increasing difficulty.
- Check the wording of the questions to make sure that there is no ambiguity.
- Carefully judge the length of the test. Pupils need to get used to completing a test in a fixed time. You may need to give extra time to pupils with learning difficulties.
- It is worth spending some time checking that the questions cover as much of the topic as is possible and that you are requiring a range of intellectual demand in the questions. You can do this by completing a grid similar to that given in Figure 8.2.
- Try to use a range of question styles from those requiring one or two word answers to those requiring one or two sentences. Include numerical questions where appropriate.
- Give due attention to the testing of literacy and numeracy.

You need to consider how frequently you are going to test pupils. It is common practice to test pupils at the end of each topic but some teachers prefer to test more often than this to keep pupils on their toes. The problem with establishing a regime of regular tests requiring recall of knowledge is that it tends to encourage rote learning.

7 | ASSESSMENT OF PRACTICAL WORK

The way in which investigative work is assessed as part of the GCSE examination has had a major influence on the way in which investigations are taught and assessed throughout the secondary school.

During KS3, teachers will want pupils to develop and extend the practical skills they have acquired in primary school, using more sophisticated apparatus or techniques. You may find it helpful for pupils to focus on certain aspects of practical work in the tasks that you set. If the pupils are doing a practical exercise that produces a lot of data you could provide them with feedback on setting out the results, the reliability of the results and manipulating the data into an appropriate graphical form. During a practical that requires them to use a measuring instrument you can give pupils guidance on how to use it accurately and let them know that during the lesson you will be checking to see that they are using it correctly. From time to time you will need to make a point about making observations during a practical task and, just as importantly, accurately recording the observations. Although some of your assessment of practical work will be through observing the pupils at work, the main method of assessment is by marking pupils' written reports. The examination boards provide teachers with a great deal of guidance on how to do this, through the specification, sample marked investigations and through INSET sessions. All examination boards have agreed to adopt the same marking system whereby pupils' work is assessed in four skill areas as shown in Figure 8.3.

The way to mark work is to read through the description for two marks, check if the statements have been met and work your way up the scale until you come to a point where the work does not meet one of the mark descriptions. Descriptions are not given for the odd marks (1, 3, 5, 7) so in order to allocate, say, a mark of 5 a pupil should satisfy all of the criteria for 4, together with some of the criteria for 6. If a pupil does not satisfy one of the 4 mark criteria but has all the 6 mark criteria, then she/he should be awarded 6 marks.

A practical activity can take the form of either experimental work or an investigation. Experimental work gives access to P, O and A skill areas. An investigation covers all four skill areas. Students must do a minimum of one investigation in the profile of marks submitted to the board. Other rules concerned with the submission of course work are summarized in Figure 8.3.

It is possible to assess individual skill areas so long as:

For P: the practical activity is appropriate to GCSE science (it must be a plausible practical, i.e. one that could have been carried out).

For O: pupils must be provided with opportunities to exercise their own judgements.

Skill area		Mark
Planning experimental procedures	P	0–8
Obtaining evidence	O	0–8
Analysing evidence and drawing conclusions	A	0–8
Evaluating evidence	E	0–6
Total		30

	Double award	Single award	For each separate science
Number of marks required	2 marks for each skill area (max. 60)	1 mark for each skill area (max. 30)	1 mark for each skill area (max. 30)
Maximum number of pieces of work from which marks can be drawn	4	2	2
Minimum number of attainment targets that must be represented	2	1	1

Figure 8.3 *Mark allocation for GCSE investigations*

For A: the results provided for analysis must be generated from real practical activities, i.e. it cannot be data made up by the teacher.

For E: the information must be provided on the procedures used including details of the equipment and method.

You will find it useful to annotate pupils' work with key words and the paragraph numbers in the specification. During the course this gives pupils valuable feedback on how to improve and on the final assessed piece of work it serves as a reminder to you as to why you allocated the marks and provides information for the moderator. It is good practice to get colleagues within a science department to cross-moderate each other's marking to check for consistency. In addition, the board will require a sample of scripts to be seen by an external moderator.

> ## *Practical activity 8.3*
>
> Familiarize yourself with the information about the assessment of practical work given in the GCSE specifications. Look at the marked examples of investigations provided by the examination board.
>
> Ask your mentor to supply you with the investigations from three pupils with the annotations and marks removed. Mark the three scripts and compare your marks to those given by your mentor.

8   ASSESSING THE NATURE OF SCIENCE

At GCSE 5 per cent of the marks on the written papers are attributed to the nature of science. Guidance on which parts of the GCSE course are appropriate for teaching and assessing this aspect are given in the science specification. The OCR specification, for example, lists the ideas about science that teachers need to present in their lessons together with teaching opportunities throughout the specification. These sorts of issues can be taught through group work and individual research projects and can lead to products that pupils could use towards a key skills certificate at levels 1 or 2 (see below and information in the science specifications).

Because of the limited amount of 'space' on the examination papers, which have to sample as much of the specification as possible, the questions are not likely to require an in depth analysis of any one issue.

9   ASSESSING THE GREY AREAS

I have grouped together those areas of the NC that teachers have a statutory obligation to teach but have no related assessment rules. These are:

- spiritual, moral, ethical and cultural dimension
- citizenship
- european dimension
- Curriculum Cymreig (in Wales).

As with the nature of science these are areas of the curriculum that provide pupils with the opportunity for producing work that could lead to key skills qualifications. For example, pupils could be asked to research topics using ICT, such as the ethical issues associated with the use of cloning or environmental issues and the role of the responsible citizen, and collect evidence that could be presented as part of their ICT portfolio. Communication skills could also be assessed through the production of a report or presentation.

10 | SELF-ASSESSMENT

Increasingly, schools are encouraging pupils to analyse their own strengths and weaknesses through the use of self-assessment forms, In one school, when a test paper is returned to pupils they are asked to identify, from a list of suggestions, the reasons why they lost marks. In the light of their analysis, they write a target for themselves (e.g. I shall read the questions more carefully and check all my calculations) and set a target mark for the next test. The self-assessment form is taken home to be counter-signed by parents, who are thus kept informed of their children's progress.

(Estyn, 2001)

A number of studies (e.g. Black and Wiliam, 1998; Torrance and Prior, 1988) have pointed to the importance of regular self-assessment in helping pupils to reflect on the way they learn and to be able to analyse the quality of their work. Black and Wiliam (1998) have shown that large improvements in performance can be achieved, particularly for low attainers, simply by getting pupils to critically review their own work.

Some primary schools are training their pupils to use self and peer group assessment and you may find that pupils will be familiar with the techniques used. For many pupils you will have to:

- explain what it means to make judgements on their own work;
- explain the term 'learning objectives';
- provide them with support and give them encouragement to carry out the assessments regularly.

Clarke (1998) suggests that teachers prepare a poster that can be displayed in the classroom displaying a group of questions that will help as a focus for pupils' reflection on their learning. She suggests the following questions:

- Do you remember the learning intention of the lesson?
- What did you find difficult?
- Did anyone or anything help you move on to learn something new (e.g. friend, equipment, resources, teacher)?
- What do you need more help with?
- What are you most pleased with?
- Did you learn anything new?

Being able to judge what they know and what they need to know is an important aspect of the learning process. It starts with the teacher making the learning objectives clear to pupils and ends with pupils monitoring their personal achievement against these objectives.

Some science textbooks encourage pupils to check their understanding by providing them with lists of what they should know at the end of each section. You can give pupils a checklist to help them review a piece of work. This will be similar to a normal teacher's mark sheet but will contain more detail to help pupils identify why they have gone wrong. You need to clearly explain to the pupils that the purpose of this procedure is to help them learn from their mistakes and give them some ideas as to what examiners want. When you ask the pupils to do a writing exercise you can ask them to suggest criteria for marking it. The discussion that follows should help them to identify the important aspects. These can be written on the board and used as a basis for self-assessment.

Pupils can 'plot' their own learning through the use of concept maps (see p. 77). This can be done easily if the key words are produced on card with reusable adhesive, e.g. Blu-Tack®, and the map itself is written in pencil. At the start of topic they can map out their prior understanding of the key concepts and as the lessons progress they can alter things or add new ideas they have learnt.

Practical activity 8.4

If you have not used self-assessment yourself, or if it is not part of the culture of the science department you are working in, it may be that you are a little concerned about trying it out for the first time.

You could start by considering how you are going to present the lesson objectives to the pupils (see p. 45) so that they understand them and can use them to check progress at various stages of the lesson. At the end of the lesson go back to the objectives and use these as a basis for your questioning and summary.

Further examples of self-assessment ideas can be found in an article by Daws and Singh (1999).

11 KEEPING RECORDS

It is important to keep accurate records of your pupils' attainment and know which type of marks you are going to use to help pupils make progress and what you will need to collect to ensure that you can compile a report at the end of term. You should also keep a check on attendance, and it is advisable to quickly make a note of who has not handed in their book for marking. This avoids the inevitable accusation from the pupil that you have lost their book.

Practical activity 8.5

Ask your mentor and other experienced teachers if you can look at the way they set out their mark books. Consider how the records:

- help the teacher to monitor the week to week progress of each pupil;
- indicate that the work was handed in late or was incomplete;
- indicate what the pupil knows (e.g. in relation to the NC PoS) and highlights gaps in knowledge;
- help the teacher to set targets;
- help the teacher to produce an end of term report.

KS National Tests	Special tasks aimed at pupils who are likely to achieve levels 1–3	Papers aimed at pupils who are likely to achieve at levels 3–6	Papers aimed at pupils who are likely to achieve levels 5–7
GCSE examination	Higher tier papers aimed at pupils who are likely to achieve A*–D		Foundation tier papers aimed at pupils who are likely to achieve C–G

Figure 8.4 *The tiered nature of KS3 and KS4 examinations*

12 | THE EXTERNAL EXAMINATIONS

At the end of year 9 all pupils have to sit the key stage 3 National Tests. These are commonly referred to as the SATS (Standard Assessment Tasks).

In preparing pupils for the National Tests you will probably feel obliged to encourage them to buy some sort of revision book to make sure that they cram in as much information as they can before the big day. The quantity and quality of examination results are what schools are judged on and, unfortunately, we are in an era when teachers feel that it is necessary to spend a lot of time preparing pupils for examinations. So you will probably find yourself going through a lot of past questions to help pupils gain a feeling for what to expect. You will need to point out to them that they will need to be very specific when writing their answers, as something that is generally correct but does not use the right words is usually marked wrong.

Teachers have to make a decision about which tier of the KS3 papers is appropriate for each pupil (see Figure 8.4). There is a special test for pupils who have not reached level 3 and two papers for each of the other tiers. Once the test has been completed, the papers are sent away to an examination board to be marked. Some time later the marked scripts are returned to the schools and a NC level is provided for each pupil. The way in which the board switches from a mark to a level is done through a system of pre-testing followed by some slight adjustments once some of the actual test scripts have been marked. Figure 8.5 shows the relationship between marks and levels for 1998 and 1999 in Wales. As you can see the level boundaries move slightly from year to year due to variation in question type and degree of difficulty.

When the whole examination process is over for the year the teacher will have a set of marked scripts, an information sheet from the board relating the marks to the levels and a report, all of which can be used to inform future teaching. The report highlights common mistakes and indicates which aspects of the NC were least understood by pupils.

There are five GCSE examination boards each offering the separate sciences, double and single science and an array of other science courses (see Figure 8.6). Departments will choose one board over another either because there is a long tradition of working with it or because they feel that the board provides better

	Mark range			
	Tier 3–6		Tier 5–7	
Level	1998	1999	1998	1999
3	40–65	33–57		
4	66–94	58–88	45–50	33–38
5	95–122	89–118	51–72	39–66
6	123+	119+	73–99	67–95
7			100+	96+

Figure 8.5 *Marks and their corresponding NC levels for the KS3 National Tests for Science in Wales for 1998 and 1999*

support for teachers than the others. Teachers may also change boards if they feel that it is easier for pupils to gain higher grades with one particular board, although in practice this should not be the case. Each specification must comply with the Science NC but each board will have developed this basic framework in different ways. You need to be careful about using past examination papers to prepare tests for pupils as the course content for GCSE has changed from time to time, and what was a perfectly good question five years ago may not be relevant to today's specification.

There are two tiers of papers (Figure 8.4) and it is up to the teacher to decide which tier is most suitable for the pupil to enter. You may find yourself in difficulties if you graded pupils' work inappropriately during the year. For example, a pupil may have an over-inflated view of his/her capabilities because

Practical activity 8.6

You will find it very useful to spend some time looking at the GCSE specification and past paper questions.

Look at the level of detail given in the specification – this will give you a good indication as to the depth of treatment you are required to cover.

Check what is on the data sheet that will be supplied to pupils in the examination. Give pupils the opportunity to use this data sheet regularly.

Study the style of the question papers and the types of questions asked. Make sure your pupils get plenty of opportunity to answer these types of questions.

	AQA www.aeb.org/uk/	CCEA www.ccea.org.uk/	Edexcel www.edexcel.org.uk/	OCR www.meg.org.uk/	WJEC www.wjec.co.uk/
Single Award Modular	✓	✓	✓	✓	✓
Double Award Modular	✓	✓	✓	✓	✓
Single Award Non-Modular	✓		✓	✓	✓
Double Aware Non-Modular	✓		✓	✓	✓
Human Biology	✓				
Suffolk Science				✓	
Salters Science				✓	

Figure 8.6 *GCSE Science Specifications offered by each of the UK Examination Boards*

Average %	85+	74–84	61–73	47–60	37–46	30–36	Under 30
Grade	A*	A	B	C	D	E	U

Figure 8.7 *The approximate relationship between GCSE grades and total percentage marks in the science papers*

you have given a long string of As for homework. It is not uncommon for parents to get very irate when their son or daughter is entered for the Foundation Tier paper when they could see from the grades you were giving that their child was excelling at science.

As with the National Tests, the grade boundaries change slightly from year to year but you can get an approximate idea of the allocation of grades using the information in Figure 8.7.

13 CURRICULUM 2000

Curriculum 2000 was a government initiative to introduce greater flexibility in learning at post-16 level and to widen the range of subjects studied. Typically, a student who is interested in following an academic science course would study four or, possibly, five AS courses in the first year of sixth form narrowing it down to three A2 courses (the second half of the A level) in the second year. The AS units are approximately half of an advanced GCE course and they lead to a qualification in their own right. A2 courses are more demanding than AS and all have one written examination that asks questions from all parts of the course (the synoptic paper). The A-level grade is calculated from both the AS mark and the A2 mark, each contributing 50 per cent.

Each unit of the course has its own externally set and marked examination but, in addition, there is a practical coursework component at both AS and A2 levels that is internally assessed and externally moderated. Each subject has two or three unit-based written examinations for both AS and A2. The examination board will generally offer opportunities to sit these exams twice a year. Students can re-sit exams to improve their grade but can only sit the exam twice.

A student who wished to follow a more vocationally oriented course would opt for the A-level Vocational Certificates of Education (VCE) units. These have a work-related emphasis and the balance of assessment is towards coursework rather than examinations. Students can mix and match VCEs with A levels. For example, a student who is thinking about nursing as a career could take Health and Social Care VCE with an A-level science. VCEs can be taken as single subjects leading to one grade or as double subjects leading to two grades.

To add greater clarity – or confusion, depending on which way you look at it – to the changing examination system a number of terms have been renamed or have been redefined as shown in Figure 8.8. The new qualification has also given rise in changes to the UCAS point system for university entrance (Figure 8.9).

Old term	New term (post 2001)
Module	Unit
Syllabus	Specification
AS (meaning Advanced Supplementary)	AS (meaning Advanced Subsidiary)
Advanced General National Vocational Qualification (GNVQ)	A-level Vocational Certificates of Education (VCE)
Special level (S level)	Advanced Extension Awards (AEA)

Figure 8.8 *Changes in examination nomenclature*

Practical activity 8.7

Obtain an advanced specification for your specialist science subject. What units are taught in the first year of the course? How is the practical coursework component organized? How does it build on the skills pupils have gained at GCSE level?

Find out from your mentor how many students only follow the course up to AS level.

Are there problems in terms of continuity of learning from GCSE to AS level?

Find out what VCE courses are available by looking at the one of the examination board's websites. Think about some of the pupils you teach at KS4 and consider what sort of courses you would advise them to do after their GCSEs.

In addition to these qualifications there are two further routes available to post-16 students in England, Wales and Northern Ireland. These are the International Baccalaureate and the Welsh Baccalaureate. Both are broad based diploma courses that require all students to study some science. Further details can be obtained from their websites at *www.ibo.org/* and *www.iwa.org.uk/news/ press_releases/pr_WelshBac_general_info.html.*

In Scotland students follow Higher or Advanced Higher courses and further details can be obtained from the Scottish Qualifications Authority web page at *www.sqa.org.uk/higher-still/.*

Key skill	GCE and VCE at AS level	GCE and VCE at A level	VCE Double Award	UCAS points
			AA	240
			AB	220
			BB	200
			BC	180
			CC	160
			CD	140
		A	DD	120
		B	DE	100
		C	EE	80
	A	D		60
	B			50
	C	E		40
Level 4	D			30
Level 3	E			20

 Figure 8.9 *The UCAS scores for advanced qualifications (for further details see the UCAS website,* www.ucas.ac.uk)

14   KEY SKILLS

Key skills are aspects of learning that are seen as being particularly valuable to employers and higher educational establishments.

The key skills are:

- application of numbers
- communication
- information technology
- improving own learning and performance
- problem solving
- working with others.

Each advanced qualification provides opportunities for students to generate evidence that they have achieved a certain standing at one of the levels. Key skills are awarded at five levels. In general, level 1 would be appropriate for students following a GCSE programme, levels 2 and 3, an advanced programme and level 4, a degree course.

Each advanced specification will show where students can work towards at key skills qualification. At present only the first three key skills in the above list contribute to the key skills qualification. This is assessed through a combination of a portfolio of evidence and an external test. These are changing all the time and it is wise to check up on the latest situation by looking at the QCA or The Learning Skills Development Agency websites (*www.qca.org.uk* and *www. lsda.org.uk/home.asp*).

Practical activity 8.8

Below are level 3 criteria from the first three key skills. Identify opportunities in your specialist subject specifications where these could be assessed:

Application of numbers

- Carry out multi-stage calculations, including use of a large data set (over 50 items) and re-arrangement of formulae.

Communication

- Read and synthesize information from extended documents about a complex subject.

Information technology

- Plan and use different sources and appropriate techniques to search for and select information based on judgements of relevance and quality.

15   THE USE OF ASSESSMENT INFORMATION

Schools have access to a great deal of data about academic performance. On a whole school basis there is the Ofsted PANDA (Performance AND Assessment) report for each school. For each pupil there is information from the key stage national tests and, usually, Cognitive Ability Tests (CATs) that can be used to predict future performance. CATs are designed to give information about pupils' ability to work things out. The results give information about the pupils under three main headings: Verbal reasoning, Non-verbal reasoning and Quantitative reasoning. The data can be used to identify specific problems that pupils may have, e.g. the conceptual nature of words, identifying number patterns, ability to deal with abstract ideas. The CATs scores can be used to predict performance in the National Tests at KS3 and at GCSE. For example, if a pupil obtains a CATs score of 100 she/he would be predicted to get a level 5 in science at KS3 and a B/C at GCSE. This doesn't mean that a pupil's examination destiny is fully mapped out for him or her, as there are many things that can be done to improve performance. Intervention programmes such as CASE, the use of specific activities to develop particular skills, matching teaching approaches to pupils' needs, improved school attendance and encouragement will all have a bearing on the examination results.

A system used in KS4 called YELLIS (**YE**ar **11** Information System) enables schools to monitor the performance of their pupils during this two-year period and compare their performance against all other pupils participating in the YELLIS scheme. One route through the system is for pupils to sit a short test in term 1 of year 10 which, when analysed, gives an indication of the potential performance in GCSE examinations and a value-added analysis at the pupil, subject and school level.

Most schools will be involved in using some sort of target setting. This might simply involve giving feedback to pupils on their written work or test result, that includes comments on how they could improve and what they should aim for next time. In other instances schools may use CATs data and/or other test data to make predictions about pupils' performance. An important aspect of using this sort of information is to make sure that pupils are aware of it and that the teacher provides them with the support to improve their grades. The overriding message must be that everyone can make progress and that the only person they are competing with is themselves. If this doesn't come across then there is a danger that less able pupils will become demotivated if their predicted GCSE score is grade D. With the right sort of help, and a positive attitude from the pupil, higher grades can be achieved. Targets need to be set on a relatively short-term basis and become part of the progress-monitoring routine.

Some schools go beyond this and use databases to track pupils' performance over all subjects. They may even use the system to compare the performance of teachers by looking at the marks achieved by pupils in comparable classes.

Practical activity 8.9

Discuss the value and the way in which some of this data is used with your mentor.

- Find out more about CATs by looking at the website (*www.nfer-nelson.co.uk/cat/*).
- What is being measured by CATs and what is being measured by the KS3 tests and GCSE examinations?
- What are the advantages and disadvantages of using CATs data to help schools group pupils into ability sets.
- How reliable is the data? Are some National Test questions biased against certain groups of pupils?
- Is there a possibility that pupils only live up to the grades predicted for them? Could pupils who have been predicted low scores become demotivated?

16 REPORTING

Reports should give a clear summary of a pupil's attainment in science and should indicate how the pupil can improve his/her performance. Although the target audience is usually the parent or guardian, you should bear in mind that the pupil will read it and, hopefully, benefit from your comments.

ACCAC have prepared the following list of key features of effective and meaningful reports. Such reports would feature:

- a focus on pupils' learning and achievements rather than what has been taught;
- the reporting of pupils' strengths and weaknesses in an unambiguous way; the aim should be to provide a balanced and objective report that makes it clear to the reader what is required of the pupil to ensure improved performance.
- the setting of well pitched and achievable targets for the pupil which the parent can support;
- comments which avoid jargon, making clear use of appropriate technical terms and use language which is readily understood by the audience;
- comments about the pupils which are individualized and subject specific, rather than bland statements;
- comments which chiefly focus on achievement but, where felt appropriate, make brief reference to a pupil's effort or attitude.

(ACCAC, 2000, p. 6)

Practical activity 8.10

Ask your mentor to have a look at some reports written for different types of pupils, e.g. high achievers, low achievers, pupils who are not fulfilling their potential, pupils with behavioural problems. Discuss with him/her:

- How do you ensure that the comments accurately reflect the abilities of the pupil?
- Do you favour a computerized system of reports over hand-written ones?
- Do you keep a bank of statements that you modify for different individuals?
- How do you identify suitable targets for pupils?
- How much should you write for each pupil?

CONCLUSION

There have been significant developments in the ways in which we collect and use assessment data in recent years. With the introduction of electronic databases it is possible to track pupils' performance in different strands of their work and identify where pupils require help. In addition, the whole process of assessment has become far more open. Teachers have a clearer picture of the requirements of examination boards and how papers are marked. Pupils know exactly what they have to learn and have staged learning objectives to help them meet their overall target. Alongside this is the growing expertise of teachers to help pupils to learn and a whole battery of resources for pupils, from online tutorials to revision guides. It's no wonder that academic standards are rising.

CHAPTER 9

Supporting progression in learning

INTRODUCTION

This chapter is about what teachers can do to help pupils make progress in their learning. Progress cannot be guaranteed in lessons as pupils sometimes stagnate or even regress if the conditions are not right. You will need to consider how you are going to provide pupils with the optimum learning environment and how you will support them in their learning.

By the end of this chapter you should:

- understand the importance of pupils' prior learning;
- be able to plan for continuity and progression in the curriculum;
- understand that pupils learn in different ways and be able to cater for this in your teaching;
- understand how information from assessment can be used to help pupils to make progress.

1 CONTINUITY OF CURRICULUM AND PROGRESSION IN LEARNING

If we want pupils to make progress in their learning of science then during their time at school they need to be exposed to a range of experiences that build on one another. In designing a teaching sequence you need to think about pupils' prior learning. What do they need to understand to be capable of learning the new topic? How are you going to consolidate previous learning? What strategies are you going to employ to move the pupils on? The process of short- and long-term planning of teaching that involves designing strategies to answer these questions is referred to as 'continuity of the curriculum'. In any one secondary school you would expect the science teachers to have sat down and worked out a curriculum, based on the NC, that provided pupils with continuity of experiences. But you need to think about continuity not just in secondary terms but also in terms of pupils' education throughout their time in school. There is a danger that secondary school teachers might choose to dismiss the fact that pupils have been taught a considerable amount of science in the primary school and repeat work during KS3. There have been many reports of this type of practice going on for what might seem to be perfectly good reasons:

- 'You can never be sure what they have covered in the primary school so it's best to start with a clean slate.'

- 'There are a lot of primary schools feeding our school and they all do something different. The only way to cope is with a fresh start.'

- 'Most of the primary school teachers aren't specialists in science and they make mistakes. It's our job to correct these.'

These types of attitude are not going to lead to continuity and it is a matter of concern that many pupils become disenchanted with science as they move through KS3 repeating some of their KS2 work.

The introduction of the NC has helped somewhat but, as it only provides the teacher with the bare bones of what should be taught, teachers sometimes interpret it in different ways, choose different examples and teach topics to different levels of difficulty. Some enthusiastic primary teachers might go well beyond the KS2 requirements in certain topics in the belief that they will be giving their pupils a head start in the secondary school.

Linked very closely to the idea of continuity of curriculum is the principle of progression in learning. Progression is about a pupil's personal learning. Providing pupils with a curriculum that supports continuity is the first step in providing progression but by itself it doesn't guarantee it. Once we have taken a look at how to reduce the problem of primary–secondary continuity we will come back to look at how to build ideas about progression into your teaching.

2 | CONTINUITY FROM PRIMARY TO SECONDARY SCHOOL

As a student teacher you are most likely teaching year 7 and other KS3 classes and therefore it is a good idea that you have some knowledge of the experiences pupils have had in their primary schools. During your induction year you may have a greater involvement in the work of year 7 and be concerned with the liaison procedures between schools. Therefore you should have some understanding of the complexity of the task and what you can do to help pupils experience a smooth transition from one education system to another.

There are a number of issues that need to be addressed in the transition process. Galton *et al.* (1999) have grouped these issues together under what they call 'bridges' that need to be crossed between the two phases of education. They have identified these as: the bureaucratic bridge; the social bridge; the curriculum bridge; the pedagogic bridge; and the management-of-learning bridge. Figure 9.1 summarizes key features of each of these. Schools do a great deal to help pupils settle in to the secondary school as quickly as possible and the number of problems that occur is generally small. As far as science is concerned, however, there can be major problems with regard to curriculum continuity as seen in the following quotations from Ofsted and Estyn reports.

Secondary school science departments are slowly adjusting to the improved scientific knowledge which pupils now have at the start of secondary schooling.

From primary	To secondary
The bureaucratic bridge	
The school has useful information on pupils such as: • assessment data • information on pupils' backgrounds • special needs information	The problems facing the secondary school are: • getting the information to the right people • using the information effectively
The social bridge	
Pupils concerned about: • being bullied in the secondary school • getting lost • the amount of homework • making friends • getting on with new teachers	To help, the school can: • have a programme of PSE lessons on bullying and an anti-bullying policy • hold induction days • provide reassurance from older pupils • plan the composition of form and teaching groups
The curriculum bridge	
The problems include: • variation in coverage and emphasis of the NC • the lack of reliability of NC teacher assessment as perceived by secondary teachers • repetition of work in the secondary school	The problems can be minimized by: • organizing cluster group meetings to exchange information and share ideas • preparing an agreed common SoW that goes across the two phases
The pedagogic bridge	
Pupils generally experience one teaching style (that of the form teacher)	Pupils have to cope with a number of different teaching styles. Some pupils find it difficult to come to terms with the different demands made on them
The management-of-learning bridge	
Pupils get used to a particular way of learning, guided by the teacher	New learning strategies are required to meet the demands of learning a wider range of subjects and increases in the level of difficulty

Figure 9.1 *Transitions between primary and secondary school*

However, there is still repetition of KS 2 work (late primary) and higher attaining pupils are insufficiently challenged.

(Ofsted, 2000, p. 7)

Science departments generally have poor liaison with the primary schools from which their pupils come. Pupils in year 7 do not always make sufficient progress beyond what they have achieved in key stage 2.

(Estyn, 2001, p. 3)

3 PUPILS' EXPERIENCES AT KEY STAGE 2

You will probably have images of what happens in primary school science lessons based on your own school experience but these may not reflect current practices. There have been considerable developments in what is taught and how it is taught. The children will be taught science concepts in much the same way as they are taught in secondary schools. There will probably be more use made of artefacts and everyday examples. There is likely to be a lot of seeing things happen and then putting forward an explanation. The work may naturally link in to other areas of the curriculum and there is a possibility that at some stage along the line it may develop into some technology work (designing and making). However, the teaching situation can change very rapidly as schools respond to government demands. During the last few years the government has given a great deal of emphasis to improving the literacy and numeracy of pupils. This has to be done at the expense of other parts of the curriculum and in many schools it has been science that has suffered. In a survey carried out by ASE (ASE, 1999) it was reported that:

- the average number of hours dedicated to science at KS1 and KS2 had declined;
- 60 per cent of the respondents were concerned about the adverse effect the literacy hour was having on science;
- 47 per cent of the respondents reported that science-based INSET (In-service Training) had been postponed due to literacy training.

Where science is done well you will find that quite a lot of emphasis is given to investigative work. The majority of these are of the fair testing type (see p. 125) and so you will expect some year 7 pupils to have significant expertise in this area.

However, you will need to take into account that the majority of year 6 teachers are non-science specialists and, although they will do everything possible to get the science correct, they will usually not have the depth of knowledge required to deal with difficult concepts. According to Osborne and Simon (1996), this lack of knowledge sometimes leads to a style of teaching involving the presentation of unrelated facts and teachers failing to understand the significance of pupils' questions. So, in some primary schools, quite understandably, teachers have difficulty in extending their pupils' knowledge. While all schools will have followed the National Curriculum, there may be considerable variation in depth of treatment.

Practical activity 9.1

Find out about how science is taught in primary schools.

Visit one or more of your school's contributory (feeder, partner) primary schools. A good time to do this is at the beginning of your period of school experience, to gain an insight into pupils' knowledge in year 6, or in the summer term when schools are carrying out liaison visits. Look at the sort of work pupils are doing and get them to talk to you about their work and what sorts of things they are looking forward to when they come to the secondary school. Talk to the teacher about what she/he does in science and the nature of the liaison with the secondary school. Ask if you can co-teach with the primary teacher. (This will need some prior planning.)

Look at past KS2 National Test papers and mark schemes and try to get a feeling for the standards achieved by pupils at different levels.

4   HELPING TO ACHIEVE CURRICULUM CONTINUITY

Even as new teachers you can make a contribution to improving the level of understanding of what goes on in the primary school and how you can build on pupils' prior learning in science. If little, or no, account is taken of pupils work at KS2 then pupils can become demotivated and disaffected with science, and repetition of work leads to a reduction in time available for the teaching of the KS3 PoS. One of the main aims of the KS3 National Science Strategy is to try to improve primary–secondary continuity and you will find it useful to look at their

published examples of good practice, *www.standards.dfes.gov.uk/keystage3/*

There are a number of ways that schools try to achieve curricular continuity across the two phases and some examples are listed below:

- By reading the programme of study for KS2, the QCA scheme of work (SoW) for KS2 (see below) and books aimed at the teaching of science to primary pupils. According to Nott and Wellington (1999), even something as simple as consulting the KS2 PoS when planning KS3 work is only carried out in a small number of schools.

- Through cluster group meetings, where the science teachers from the secondary school meet with the science co-ordinators from the contributory primary schools to discuss how they can help one another. At these meetings they could formulate a common SoW identifying what will be taught in each sector. Secondary school teachers could help with the understanding of science concepts. Although there may be initial embarrassment from primary colleagues about gaps in their knowledge it is possible to overcome this by starting the discussion around the detail of the work to be covered for a topic.

- By KS2 and KS3 teachers working together to produce a topic workbook (e.g. on forces and motion) that is used in the primary school and then completed in the secondary school.

- Through discussions on standards of pupils' work in KS2 using the National Tests and teacher assessment as the starting point.
- By visiting one another's schools to gain first hand experience of how things are taught.
- By secondary teachers carrying out revision lessons with year 6 pupils prior to them sitting the National Tests.
- By coming to an agreement on what sort of data should be transferred from the primary to the secondary school and to whom it should go. The primary school might also welcome feedback on the progress of pupils in the secondary school.

Progress on cross phase curriculum continuity has been painstakingly slow and, as pointed out by Stephenson (1999), even after ten years of a five to sixteen National Curriculum we are still experiencing substantial discontinuity. Perhaps one of the ways forward is for you, the new generation of teachers, to make a difference.

Practical ctivity 9.2

Through your science mentor examine the way the school organizes continuity of the curriculum.

Find out what information is transferred from the primary school and what is done with the information. Are the KS2 National Test results used for grouping pupils in year 7? Is the teacher assessment data used?

With your mentor devise a few questions to ask pupils in each of the KS3 years about their likes and dislikes about science. Clearly, there are other factors that can contribute to a drop in motivation during KS3 such as changes in home background, relationships and the maturation process. Consider what could be done to improve the science curriculum in KS3. (You could think about things such as style of teaching across the KS, the degree of intellectual challenge posed to pupils at various stages, the pattern of the curriculum.)

5   HELPING PUPILS TO MAKE PROGRESS

Up to now we have been talking about the things that a teacher can do to provide pupils with a continuity of experiences. Now we are going to turn to the idea of progression which is more concerned with pupils' personal learning and development. Progression isn't just about learning more and more things, it is also about learning in depth, being able to deal with more complex situations and more abstract concepts. Figure 9.2 outlines three broad areas in which progression can take place. In order to help pupils to make progress you need to have a curriculum that will support progression and a knowledge of pupils' current level of understanding. At various times in a pupil's school career the

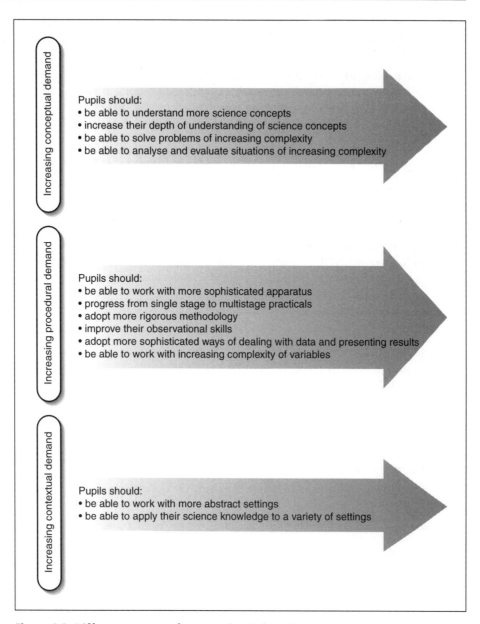

Figure 9.2 *Different aspects of progression in learning*

rate of learning can slow down or even go into reverse. There are all sorts of reasons for this from things that are going on at home or with friends to problems with the subject. The problems could be a difficulty in understanding or the pupil finding the work too easy. More able pupils can easily become disaffected and disruptive if they are not sufficiently challenged. Your job is to encourage the pupil and to provide work at an appropriate level. Some ideas about how you might achieve this are described in the next section.

6 DIFFERENTIATION

The process of catering for pupils of different abilities is called differentiation. A differentiated approach to teaching will help pupils make progress in their learning. The starting point for your planning for differentiation must be the realization that in your class of 30 or so pupils you have considerable variation in:

- preferred way of learning (see multiple intelligences, p. 18)
- motivation to learn
- ability to learn.

Many experienced teachers apply some sort of differentiation without really thinking about it. They can do this because they know their class well and can alter their teaching to meet the pupils' needs. You will need to build up your expertise and will only be able to do it effectively once you know the capabilities of the individuals in your classes.

The following list shows the characteristics of differentiated teaching (adapted from NIAS, 1995):

- a knowledge of an individual's prior understanding;
- clearly defined learning objectives for all pupils and for pupils of different ability;
- the use of a range of learning resources and/or activities;
- opportunities for pupils to work at different paces;
- the teacher working briefly with many individuals;
- little whole class teaching;
- pupils being aware of what they are doing and being able to make some decisions about their own learning;
- individual comments made on pupils' work to help them to make progress.

As a student teacher you need to think about strategies that will enable you to build up some sort of differentiated teaching. For example, you can target your questioning to individuals based on your knowledge of how capable the pupil is at giving you an answer. Simple recall questions would be asked of the less able and more complex questions directed to the more able.

Some publishers provide differentiated science textbooks, e.g. the Eureka series for KS3 (Chapman et al., 2000). These books look very similar from the outside except that one has green markings (a foundation level book) and one has red markings (a higher level book). The books contain parallel double page spreads to cover the content but the structure and layout of the books are different. In the green book there is less text, the print size is larger and the language is simplified. In the red book, the text and content is more challenging and the questions more demanding.

You could use some of these ideas when you prepare worksheets. You might consider preparing two different levels of a worksheet that you distribute to appropriate pupils in a class. In some classes pupils are used to receiving different instructional materials but in others they may not be and you will have to be sensitive not to cause embarrassment to the less able. A slightly different approach is to use graded exercises where everyone is able to do some of the work and the more able have the opportunity to complete more demanding work.

Figure 9.3 provides you with a number of other examples that you could use. You need to be aware that there are different levels at which you can tackle differentiation and these are illustrated in Figure 9.4. You will, hopefully, develop your ability to cater for the needs of individuals over the first few years of your teaching experience. The process of learning is likely to be most effective when it is valued by pupils and they know what they have to do for themselves. A teacher who is good at differentiation would incorporate effective strategies into both his/her long- and short-term planning and establish routines that encourage pupils to become independent learners.

So far we have been looking at differentiation by giving pupils different sorts of things to do, this is called 'differentiation by task'. Another way of looking at it is to give everyone the same task, knowing that some pupils will be able to get much further with it than others. This is called 'differentiation by outcome'. You can immediately see the problem with this second approach as low ability pupils may be unable to make much headway with the task and may quickly become demotivated. However, with open tasks, such as some investigations, it is possible to use the differentiation by outcome approach.

Practical activity 9.3

Plan a lesson that involves you using differentiated learning techniques and then review your teaching of the lesson by answering the following questions:

- How did you make judgements about the pupils' abilities?
- How did you make judgements about the level of difficulty of the work?
- Did you choose to give the abler pupils more work to do (quantity of work) or more difficult work?
- How well did the pupils get on with their tasks? Did they appear to enjoy the work? Did they show interest and ask you questions?
- How could you improve your differentiated approach?
- What do you see as the advantages and disadvantages of each of the examples of differentiation given in this chapter (see Kerry and Kerry, 1997 and Hall, 1997, for teachers' comments)?

7 | TARGET SETTING

Target setting is an initiative set up by the DfEE for improving schools. It is based on the principle that some schools are not as effective as others in helping pupils to maximize their ability. At the whole school level there could be targets related to a variety of things, such as: increasing the percentage of pupils

Questioning	Direct questions to particular individuals trying to match the level of difficulty of the question with the pupil's ability to answer. Think about this when planning the lesson. Give praise for trying as well as for getting the right answer. Try to develop a climate where individuals feel valued. Encourage pupils to ask questions or get them to write down questions related to the topic.
Pupils' writing	Look for different ways of getting pupils to express their ideas. Some pupils may not be able to write as much as others but may still have good ideas about science. Consider using writing frames (with suggestions as to what sort of thing to write about). More able pupils may say that they no longer need them. Provide pupils with a copy of the key words you want them to use.
Pace	Consider how you are going to cater for different speeds of working. Think about your speed of delivery and the length of time you talk. Less able pupils may finish tasks early because they feel that they can't do the work so they give up or they may take a longer time. You need to be aware of this and provide appropriate help and encouragement. More able pupils may not respond positively to being given extra things do if they finish early so you need to think about how you could alter the task to make it more demanding from the start.
Assessment	Look for signs of effort as well as achievement. It is easy to come to the conclusion that a piece of work is poor because the presentation is poor. With low ability pupils try to look beyond the poor spelling and grammar for an understanding of the science. Give praise and encouragement. Provide guidance on how the pupil could improve. Don't restrict this to comments on presentation.
Investigations	You can give all the class the same topic to investigate but direct different groups to carry it out in different ways. With less able groups you may want a simple qualitative approach but with more able you might want a quantitative approach and the use of derived variables. You may also differentiate in terms of the type of equipment you expect them to use, the degree of precision of the readings you expect them to make and the number of repeat readings you expect.
Activities	Check through your lesson plans to make sure that you are providing the pupils with a variety of activities over a period of time. Consider using open-ended activities such as concept maps just to see how much the pupils can achieve. Consider setting different tasks to different groups of pupils, perhaps using different resources. Collect information from each of the groups towards the end of the lesson to build up the whole picture.

Figure 9.3 *Some ideas for a differentiated approach to teaching*

http://www.rtweb.info

The teacher:
- uses group work and varies the task dependent on the ability of the group;
- considers the level of difficulty of his/her oral questions and asks pupils appropriately;
- keeps an eye on pupils' marks, identifies underachievement and takes action;
- ensures that a variety of tasks are used in the teaching of any one topic

The teacher:
- makes sure that s/he talks to as many individual pupils as possible duing the lesson;
- encourages pupils to take some responsibility for planning their own learning;
- makes effective use of extension material given in pupils' textbooks;
- provides resources (e.g. books, CD-ROMs) for individual work both in and out of lesson time

The teacher:
- plans for differentiation through the SoW and lesson plans;
- has clear objectives for different ability groups;
- prepares different resources to match the needs of the ability groups;
- uses numerical data e.g. CATS results as a baseline for monitoring pupils' progress. Ensures that pupils work to achieve their target

Increasing the level of differentiation

Figure 9.4 *A range of approaches to differentiation (each level incorporates the principles given in the lower levels)*

achieving A*–C at GCSE; improving attendance rates; improving the school facilities. Individual subject departments will also have targets and these will usually be related to those of the whole school. If these are academic or pastoral targets then it will be the responsibility of the individual teachers to make sure that they are achieved.

In order for targets to be useful they need to be clearly written and match the principles outlined in the acronym, SMART:

Specific	e.g. increase the number of investigations in year 7 from three to five
Measurable	i.e. involve numerical values
Achievable	need to take into account a whole range of school factors
Realistic	e.g. judged by comparing performance with other departments
Time-related	i.e. set a deadline.

Let's say that a science department's target is to increase the number of pupils gaining grade C or above in Double Award Science from 53 per cent to 58 per cent. A time would have to be set by which they would hope to achieve this target and they would have to consider how they were going to do it. It is likely that the department would opt for a two-year period for this sort of turn around and they may consider some, or all, of the following procedures:

- the identification of those pupils who are on the C–D borderline in order that they can be targeted for extra help;

- a review of the KS4 SoW to check for compatibility with the syllabus and the time allotted for different topics and activities;

- a review of the resources available for learning;
- a review of the procedures for setting homework;
- a review of the marking policy;
- to consider how to improve pupils' motivation, behaviour and attitude towards science;
- how to improve attendance;
- how pupils could be made to be more responsible for their own learning.

Having targets and procedures that have been agreed upon means that each teacher needs to consider how she/he is going to work to help meet these goals. Figure 9.5 outlines some of the things an individual teacher could do through a review of two of the procedures from the above list.

You have got to be sensible about target setting and make sure that you don't set up situations that are going to be extremely stressful for all concerned. A little stress is fine, and the knowledge that we have something to aim for that requires a little bit more effort than we are currently putting in can be exciting, and can have considerable additional benefits once achieved. In setting targets it is important to talk to individual pupils and think about how you are going to raise their expectations; promote their self-esteem and self-confidence; and be realistic about their potential for achieving the targets (Lawley, 1999).

Here are some suggestions for using a target-setting approach:

- Working with individuals, set short-term goals one at a time. Don't overburden a pupil.
- Require pupils to set medium to long term goals for themselves.
- Give rewards for achieving targets.
- Convert test scores into a NC level or GCSE grade for pupils.
- Keep your marks on a spreadsheet so that you can easily make calculations and do tracking exercises.
- Compare test mark profiles with other science teachers.

Target setting can become just another administrative chore to do or it can make a real difference to pupils' performance and the whole culture of learning within a school. Improvement in performance is not brought about by simply setting targets – it requires the teacher and the pupil to work on strategies for raising standards.

Practical activity 9.4

Find out how the department's targets fit in with whole school targets.

Target setting can be used to compare teachers within a department (Teacher A's pupils always achieve their targets while in teacher B's classes there are a significant number of pupils who don't) and one department with another. Consider the effect this might have on individuals and departments.

Homework procedures	
What can you do to make sure that all pupils hand in their work on time? What punishment do you have for those that don't?	Have a regular routine. Let the pupils know that you are serious about homework. Hold a lunchtime detention for those who don't hand in their work.
What do you do about marking homework?	Make sure that you mark all homework as this conveys the message that you value it. Some will need detailed marking and others will not.
What type of homework should you set?	The homework should be sufficiently interesting for the pupils to want to do it. It should give them an opportunity to consolidate what they have learnt in class or for them to find out things for themselves. Increasingly at KS4 pupils should do typical GCSE questions.
Marking policy	
What are you going to give credit for: neatness, correct spelling and use of grammar, completeness, effort, correct use of science, etc.?	You must choose a system that is meaningful both to you and to the pupil. Your main aim is to improve pupils' understanding of science and therefore this should be the key factor in your marking. You can include written comments about other aspects of their work. Let the pupils know what they are going to be assessed on.
How do you get pupils to improve?	You can set them targets or you can negotiate targets with them. Use a range of targets from improving neatness to getting a higher mark on the next homework or test.
How do you monitor improvement?	You need to keep accurate records and periodically check individual's progress. Compare similar pupils and find out why one pupil is not making the progress you had hoped for.

Figure 9.5 *Teacher actions to achieve targets for improvement in pupils' perform-ance at KS4*

8 THE USE OF ASSESSMENT INFORMATION

When you are marking a piece of work you may spot where pupils have clearly misunderstood what has been taught. When you mark a test you may notice that groups of pupils have got one particular question wrong. It is not always correct to assume that because pupils have got things wrong in a test they didn't revise thoroughly enough. If more than just one or two pupils have got things wrong then it is quite likely that something was not quite right with your teaching. So you need to evaluate the situation, look back at your lesson plans, and try to work out what went wrong. This is using assessment in its evaluative sense.

Alternatively, your teaching may have been brilliant with clear explanations and lots of examples but the pupils simply failed to make the links you expected. Your first job is to try to diagnose where the problem lies. It could be that they have interpreted what your said in the wrong way or it could be that they have misunderstood some previous work that has an impact on the learning of this new topic. Here you are using assessment in its diagnostic sense in determining problems in pupils' learning.

In both these situations pupils are going to need your support if they are to make progress. Sometimes this may involve re-teaching the piece of work, i.e. following the right hand loop in Figure 9.6. You also need to learn from this experience and make the necessary adjustments the next time you teach the topic. Or it may involve giving feedback to pupils as to what they have done wrong and how they should correct it. This is using assessment in its formative sense.

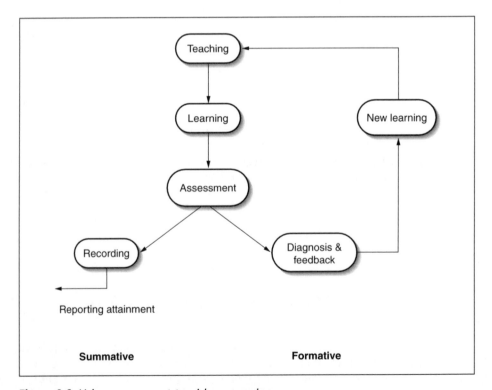

Figure 9.6 *Using assessment to aid progression*

Practical activity 9.5

Mark a class set of books and provide pupils with formative assessment where appropriate. Tell the pupils that you want them to have followed up on your comments by a particular deadline. (The sort of things they might need to do could be: correct some science, find out more information to make the exercise complete, include some additional relevant work.) After the deadline check to see that they have made the necessary improvements. What will you do if they haven't?

CONCLUSION

Science is one of those linear subjects where new knowledge builds on previous knowledge and when the original foundations are poor there is the danger that the whole lot will crumble. You need to be aware of the problems that face teachers in providing continuity of the curriculum. At first these may seem daunting and almost impossible to achieve but with some careful planning and thoughtful teaching it is possible to provide pupils with the sorts of experiences that will help them to expand their understanding of science.

CHAPTER 10

Making science appeal to all pupils

INTRODUCTION

This chapter will examine the learning needs of different groups of pupils. It will, hopefully, raise your awareness of the learning needs of pupils with different backgrounds and abilities. Science has no barriers; it is open to all pupils to learn as much as they can learn. It is of value to all, from helping each and everyone to understand and cope with things on a daily basis to pushing forwards the frontiers of knowledge. Science should be a subject that all pupils enjoy. They should find it stimulating and feel challenged about finding things out.

By the end of this chapter you should:

- understand the importance of providing work to match the needs of the pupils;

- appreciate the value of tolerance and be able to encourage pupils to adopt a tolerant outlook of others;

- know about providing resources and teaching methods to meet different situations.

1   GROUPING PUPILS FOR LEARNING

Pupils are grouped in schools in different ways, mainly either in subject sets or in mixed ability groups. The reasons for choosing one particular method are complex and take into account a host of different factors, such as:

- matching the curriculum to pupils' ability;

- behaviour and class management problems;

- ease of teaching and teacher satisfaction;

- pupils' self-esteem and happiness;

- improving examination results and the position of the school in the league tables.

In a completely mixed ability class you would expect to find pupils with the potential to go on to study at university being taught alongside pupils who have difficulties with reading and writing. In some schools the range of ability in any one class is narrowed down by dividing the year group into two or three ability bands. Mixed ability teaching tends to be more demanding on the teacher in terms of thinking about the needs of pupils and employing differentiated techniques. Some teachers may try to take the easy route and teach to pupils in the middle of the ability range with the hope that the less able will learn something and that the most able will make further progress by themselves. If you look at the issue in terms of ease of matching the curriculum to pupils' ability then grouping pupils in sets looks like the best option. This also appears to be the government's preferred choice:

> It [mixed ability grouping] requires excellent teaching and in some schools it has worked well. But in too many cases it has failed both to stretch the brightest and to respond to the needs of those who have fallen behind. Setting, particularly in science, maths and languages, is proving effective in many schools. We do not believe that any single model of grouping pupils should be imposed on secondary schools, but unless a school can demonstrate that it is getting better results through a different approach, we do make the assumption that setting should be the norm in secondary schools.
>
> (DfEE, 1997, p. 38)

This, however, does not match up with a lot of the research on pupil grouping, which states that placing pupils in sets has no significant effect on their performance (Ireson *et al.*, 1999). In addition to academic results, schools also have to consider the effects on pupils' morale and discipline. Not surprisingly pupils in low sets tend to have a poor attitude towards the subject and a low level of self-esteem. Setting also reinforces the segregation of pupils in terms of social class, gender, race and age (season of birth). The result of this is that low ability groups tend to contain a disproportionately large number of pupils from working-class backgrounds, boys, pupils from ethnic minorities and summer born children (Sukhnandan and Lee, 1998).

The grouping situation that a school or a department adopts will depend on a consideration of academic, social and philosophical factors and you may find you have some sort of mixed arrangement.

Practical activity 10.1

How does your school science department group pupils for teaching purposes: mixed ability, broad ability bands, or sets? Find out why the department chooses to group pupils in this way.

How does the science department cater for pupils of different abilities? What sort of resources are available? Do teachers specialize in teaching specific types of groups?

2 | TEACHING PUPILS WITH SPECIAL EDUCATIONAL NEEDS

Science can offer a great deal to pupils with learning difficulties and you will generally find these pupils enjoy their science lessons. Like all young people they like finding out about things, particularly things associated with their daily lives. They enjoy practical work and can frequently participate on the same level as pupils who are more able than themselves. You can add to their enjoyment by designing the work so that the amount of writing they have to do is fairly limited. The depth of science someone with learning difficulties is likely to remember will be fairly limited but the ongoing experiences of science should leave the pupils with a sense of wonder about the world and an understanding about how scientists find things out.

Schools follow a well-defined procedure in the identification of pupils with learning difficulties and the planning of suitable learning experiences for them, called the Code of Practice. The Code identifies the responsibilities of teachers, parents and the LEA in helping the child to make progress. The process can go through up to five stages (Figure 10.1) depending on the level of difficulty and ability of the school to meet the pupil's needs. The Code stresses the importance of parental involvement at every stage and, whenever possible, the views of the child. From stage 2 onwards a planning document called an Individual Education Plan (IEP) is drawn up. An IEP will:

Stage	Process	Who organizes?
1	Subject teacher or form tutor identifies that a pupil has special education needs. The SENCO is consulted. Advice is given to teachers.	School
2	The SENCO co-ordinates the special provision for the pupil. An IEP is drawn up.	School
3	Existing arrangements are reviewed and IEP revised. The SENCO consults outside agencies (e.g. an educational psychologist).	School
4	The LEA considers if a statutory assessment should be made based on all the evidence from school and home.	School and LEA
5	Based on the assessment the LEA considers if a statement of special education needs should be made. The existing arrangements are reviewed and new provision considered.	School and LEA

Figure 10.1 *The five-stage process for reviewing pupils' special educational needs*

http://www.rtweb.info

- identify the pupil's strengths and needs;
- identify specific, achievable and measurable targets;
- provide success criteria within a specific timescale;
- identify the provision, including the length and frequency, of the support;
- clarify the monitoring arrangements.

Pupils have many different forms of learning difficulties and you will find it extremely beneficial to liaise with the school's Special Educational Needs Coordinator (SENCO) to determine the nature of the pupil's individual needs. As a teacher, you will gradually build up a picture of pupils' strengths and weaknesses and, from time to time, you may note that a pupil is in need of further support for a particular skill. The sorts of things you would be looking for in order to identify pupils with learning difficulties are:

- Pupils who have difficulty in learning from conventional teaching at any one time. They stand out in the class as pupils who don't understand or who are not able to master particular skills.
- Pupils who need to repeat new learning before they are able to retain the information. They need to have more practice in using the information before they can generalize from the learning experience. They have difficulty in building things up into a logical sequence.
- Pupils may exhibit some or all of the following characteristics: poor handwriting, poor spelling, poor presentation of work, frequent loss of work, forgetting pens, etc.
- Pupils lack confidence in their own ability and will need to ask for help for the simplest of things. They will look for reassurance that they are doing things right.
- Pupils may have a long background of experiencing failure and may have low self-esteem. As a result of this they may have behaviour or emotional problems.

A key feature of helping these pupils is to help them to build their own confidence and self-esteem by providing them with achievable tasks and giving them praise for trying hard. Clearly, you need to be sensitive to their feelings and much of the support and feedback you give individuals will be on a one-to-one basis. One way of building their self-esteem is to make sure that you include them when you ask pupils to carry out jobs for you, e.g. handing out of books or equipment, taking the register back to the office. You can also allocate a specific role for them in group situations, one where they are able to develop their oral skills in a less threatening group environment and not one that requires them to write a great deal.

When preparing written materials for the pupils you need to use strategies such as:

- writing in a larger font size;
- using pictorial or diagrammatic representations;
- reducing the print density on the page.

The work needs to be broken down into small, achievable tasks and you may decide to separate these out clearly on the sheets or give the pupils sections to complete one at a time. You also need to bear in mind that the final product must 'look good' in the same way that you would expect work to be presented for high ability pupils.

Pupils are likely to require a lot of support with their writing. They may have difficulty reading things from the board and transcribing the information to their sheets, particularly if there are several lines of writing. This problem can be overcome by supplying pupils with the information on sheets and asking them to write sentences in their own words or complete a cloze type exercise. They are not going to learn a great deal of science through copying and you may find that such work acts as a disincentive to study the subject. Further ideas for teaching science to pupils with special needs are given in Parkinson (1994, p. 182).

Most schools employ support teachers to assist pupils with special needs by helping them to read or write during the lesson. By talking briefly to these people about the aims of your lesson and what you would like these children to achieve, you can release yourself from some of the mechanics of dealing with these children. You may find that if you don't adequately brief the assistant then things may happen which are detrimental to the pupil's learning. For example, you may find that the assistant does the work for the child or tells the child the answers to the questions rather than giving the child the opportunity to think.

When you first mark work from pupils with learning difficulties you may be tempted to correct everything that is incorrect, leaving a mass of red ink over the page. This can be very off-putting and is not likely to lead to any learning. A better approach is to focus on key aspects of the work and give credit for that. Look out for pupils who don't use the correct, formal language to describe a situation but instead use terms that are familiar to them. They may have gone a long way to understanding the concept but don't have the vocabulary to get their ideas across. In addition to the tiered papers mentioned above and tasks

Practical activity 10.2

How does your school make provision for pupils with the following disabilities:

- autism;
- emotional and behavioural difficulties (EBD);
- deafness;
- visual impairment;
- speech, language and communication difficulties;
- physical disabilities?

In what ways does the science curriculum for pupils with learning difficulties differ from that offered to the main group of pupils?

What could you do to enable pupils to use scientific terms correctly?

rather than tests for levels 1 and 2 (Swain, 1996), special arrangements for the testing of pupils at the end of KS3 can be made for pupils with certain physical disabilities. For example, it is possible to have Braille or enlarged print versions of the test papers or, if it is more appropriate, a reader or an amanuenses can be used.

3 | TEACHING THE MORE ABLE PUPILS

There are always a number of pupils in schools who can be categorized as being more able. These are pupils with a high potential ability in certain specific areas and, by effective teaching, these can be developed resulting in considerable achievement (O'Brien, 2000). In addition to this group of pupils, you may have some with special talents or gifts and those who are all round academically high achievers. You can identify the more able pupils, not just through their academic results but by the characteristics they display in lessons (Clark and Callow, 1998). These characteristics include:

- speed of information processing;
- highly efficient memory;
- ability to see patterns and make connections;
- intellectual curiosity.

Science has the capacity to offer these pupils considerable stimulus and engagement in tasks that will benefit their development. In fact if they are not suitably challenged, not only will it be a disappointing waste of their time but it could result in the pupils being disillusioned with science and becoming disruptive. These pupils may, quite naturally, want to go beyond the curriculum set for their age range. You could do this by directing them to more advanced books or by spending some time with them explaining the concepts at a higher level. Another effective way is to involve them in a lunchtime, or after school, science club where they can meet with other like-minded pupils, including some older ones. It is also important to create opportunities for these pupils to look at the work in depth. This involves pupils using the knowledge and skills they have learnt and applying them to different situations to solve problems. Further benefit can be gained from the task by asking them to analyse how they tackled the problem and what did they learn from the experience. In a practical situation the pupils can be challenged about the accuracy and validity of the experiment and how best to represent the results.

Peer pressure also applies to these young people and they don't want to stand out as 'swots'. By creating the right sort of environment in your classroom you can provide opportunities for the more able child to use their higher-order thinking skills without making it a big deal. While some pupils will prosper on having to do extra work and will welcome it, others may be put off if they see that they are required to spend additional time on homework and cannot see the reason for doing it.

Practical activity 10.3

Find out more about teaching more able children by visiting the website for the National Association for Able Children in Education (NACE at *www.nace.co.uk*).

Problem solving is a significant aspect of a scientist's work and can be numerical, situational, or practical.

- Try to identify when you asked your pupils to solve problems during the last week.
- What does your result tell you about the way in which you are presenting science to your pupils?
- What do you think is important to include in your instructions when devising writing tasks for the more able pupil?

4 SCIENCE CLUBS

Science clubs can provide the basis for a good social mix of pupils. While some pupils will come along with clear ideas about what they want to do you may find that the majority have no clear focus, except that they want to do experiments that are more dangerous than the ones they do in class. It is a good idea to give the pupils some clear direction as to what they are able to do in the club and what the ground rules are. It's best not to leave it wide open, otherwise you will spend a lot of time sorting things out and very little will be achieved. You may find it helpful to have a set number of activities that pupils work round over a period of time. Another possibility is to get pupils to work on activities related to a national organization such as the Salters' Chemistry Club or the BAYS (British Association of Young Scientists) network of science clubs.

5 GENDER ISSUES

Gender issues in education frequently feature in the press (Figure 10.2) and over the last few years there has been significant interest in the under achievement of boys, particularly at the GCSE stage. It is a complex issue, covering all aspects of the curriculum, teaching methods and assessment techniques. One of the dangers in dealing with the issue is to over generalize and forget that there is a wide variation in terms of ability and aptitude within both boys and girls.

Before the introduction of a compulsory science national curriculum there was considerable concern about the small number of girls studying physics at GCSE level and the lack of boys studying biology. This problem 'disappeared' once all pupils were required to study science up to the age of 16 and the focus of teachers' attention turned towards pupils' achievement. On a year-by-year basis, girls outperform boys. This is very significant for all subjects except for

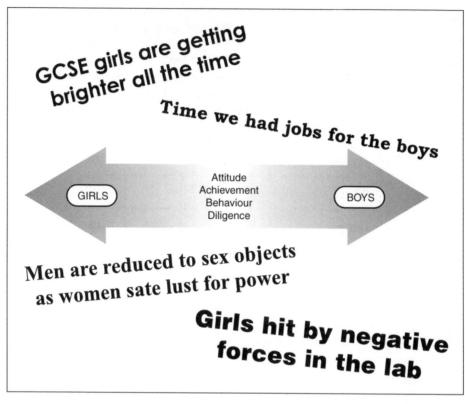

Figure 10.2 *The academic differences between boys and girls often hit the news-paper headlines*

maths and science where the margins tend to be quite small (Figure 10.3). When you begin to delve a little deeper into the science results you can identify differences between the genders. Girls tend to lack confidence in their own ability and, as a result, more girls than boys are entered for the lower tier paper. Boys tend to outperform girls on questions that require the application of physics concepts. Girls may obtain higher marks in their written reports of their investigations, as they tend to perform better than boys in tasks that require extended writing. Girls also tend to take greater care over the presentation of their work and this may have some influence on the marker.

It is when you begin to look at pupils' attitudes towards science that you begin to see differences that have a major impact on what pupils do once the science subjects become optional. From a very early age we begin to acquire certain views about what we like and what we dislike. Roles for boys and girls can start to develop before pupils start their compulsory schooling. Girls frequently enjoy creative activities such as reading a book, drawing and talking. Many boys are happier being involved in some sort of building activity. These built-in mental models are bound to influence how individuals react to the situations they find themselves in during their science lessons. They may see things from different perspectives, be able to think things through in different ways and respond more effectively in different formats. Boys tend to enjoy

Subject	Percentage of pupils achieving A*–C			
	1996		2000	
	Boys	Girls	Boys	Girls
Mathematics	46	46	49	50
English	48	65	51	66
Double Award Science	48	49	49	52
French	41	55	42	58
Geography	50	56	55	61
History	52	60	58	64

Figure 10.3 *GCSE results for all pupils from two years showing the variation in achievement between boys and girls (source: DfES, www.dfes.gov.uk/statistics)*

practical work more than girls. Sometimes they adopt an almost aggressive approach to practical work, grabbing what they would consider to be the best apparatus and pushing aside classmates who want to join in. In a mixed sex group doing an experiment you may find it is the boys that do the hands-on work while the girls sit and watch. Poor behaviour from the boys may mean that the teacher's attention is directed more at them and as a result the girls get less of the teacher's time. Throughout their time in school, girls tend to favour biology over the other sciences and boys tend to favour physics. You may see this by looking at the gender balance in post-16 courses. First, you may see that large numbers of females have chosen not to study science beyond GCSE and those that have tend to choose biology. The situation is repeated when pupils make their choice of degree courses, with all the sciences, except biological science, being dominated by men and all the arts courses dominated by women. It could be argued that science is loosing a large proportion of very able people to other subjects because of its failure to present the subject in a positive light at school. As science brings tremendous benefits to us all it is worth considering how we might try to generate a more positive attitude towards science from an early age. The key is to have a strategy that involves the highest expectations and demands the highest standards from both boys and girls and to put on one side the assumptions we have about gender stereotypes. The following list of suggestions may help to alleviate the problems.

- Bearing in mind pupils' learning preferences, try to ensure that you use a range of activities in your lessons. Use group discussion and other activities involving pupil talk in addition to practical tasks. Consider the length of time for tasks. Boys tend to have less patience than girls and may wish to move on to something new.

- When you carry out a question and answer session try to make sure that the questions are evenly distributed between the boys and the girls. Curb individuals or groups who want to dominate the situation. You may, for example, have a boy with a particular interest in the topic who wants to expand on your presentation of the subject matter. This could go on for some time and result in some pupils switching off. While you don't want to discourage pupils to show interest in this way, you need to be sensitive to the needs of all your pupils. In this instance it may be more appropriate to make arrangements for the pupil to talk to you about his interest at another time.

- Encourage all pupils to be actively involved in the work you set them. Don't allow any pupil to be sidelined. Wherever possible, try to think of ways of doing this through the instructions you give the pupils rather than having to chivvy them up as you go round.

- Think about the context that you use to present science concepts and try to choose a variety that will appeal to both boys and girls.

- Be explicit about the value of science and its cross-cultural dimension. Wherever possible relate the work you are doing to everyday examples and topical issues.

- Listen carefully to what pupils say as they may be looking at a science concept from a different perspective. You can do a lot of damage to a pupil's confidence by devaluing what she/he says, particularly when they have put a great deal of thought and effort in coming to the conclusion.

- You need to be aware of peer pressure, particularly the pressure amongst boys not to work. The pupils need to be put in situations where they have no option but to work. Boys may need to be helped/taught to organize their work.

- Seating pupils in a boy–girl arrangement may help learning and behaviour.

Practical activity 10.4

Look at the GCSE results for last year for your school and compare the percentages of boys and girls achieve five A*–C grades in a range of subjects. Look at the science entry for that year and compare the number of pupils entered for each tier in terms of gender.

Compare the GCSE coursework marks for boys and girls for last year's cohort.

How many boys and girls are doing each of the sciences at post-16 level?

Prepare and administer a short questionnaire to find out why pupils have opted to study science post-16 and what they intend to do with their science qualification once they leave school.

6 | MULTICULTURAL ISSUES

In the case of multiculturalism it is a little more difficult to pinpoint what the issues are for science teaching. On a whole school basis you would expect to have some sort of policy statement on the topic describing the school's position on discrimination and racial prejudice. This should apply to all schools irrespective of their ethnic mix. This is obvious when the school has pupils from a wide range of cultural backgrounds but some schools, with a mainly white population, have been slow in introducing a policy. It is no use schools ignoring the situation, believing that because the school is effectively 'mono-cultural' there is no problem (Gaine and George, 1999). All young people are going to have to live and work in a multi-cultural society and it is up to the school to prepare pupils for this situation. Pupils need to be taught about the differences within our society otherwise they will tend to have a very narrow perspective on life and believe that their views are the correct ones. Some pupils can be very cruel and are prepared to pick on any difference a pupil has from the 'norm', whether it be height, weight, type of clothes or colour of skin. Such prejudice can lead to bullying. It is the job of all teachers to counter any attempts by pupils to make racist comments and to explain why it is offensive. Offensive graffiti should be removed immediately and the perpetrator dealt with. You may be one of those people who thinks that jokes based on perceived cultural or national traits about people are perfectly acceptable. Perhaps you may think that such banter can diffuse a situation. In any situation you need to think very carefully of the effect it will have on the audience – in my view, such jokes are best avoided.

There are a number of things, in particular, that science can contribute to pupils' understanding of multicultural issues. There are plenty of opportunities in science teaching to stress the importance of tolerance and the appreciation of other people's point of views. Scientists are judged on the value of their work and not on their personality, the quality of their English or their cultural background. We need to get the message across that science has benefited considerably from the contributions of scientists from all over the world. It is truly a multicultural subject. A large number of pupils place great store in the high technology of the leading nations and cast disparaging remarks about so called 'low tech' countries. In science we can make the point that the technology has to suit the prevailing conditions in the particular country and that technologies need to be evaluated in terms of the effects they have on the environment.

There are opportunities when studying the topic of variation to consider the term 'race' by examining the variation in characteristics across a class in terms of tongue rolling ability, eye colour, hand span, etc. This could be extended to look at the importance of differences within a society and arguments about cloning.

All modern science textbooks adopt a multicultural approach and use a cross-section of images of people and situations to be found in the UK. When you select a textbook to use with a class you should spend some time considering what sort of underlying messages are being transmitted by the text. When you use the book with a class, listen carefully to pupils' reactions and consider when it might be appropriate to follow up their remarks or observations. Thankfully, the number of young people with extreme racial views is decreasing. But there is still a small but significant band of people who, mainly through a lack of understanding, are hostile to different ethnic groups.

Pupils who have recently come to this country and pupils whose home language is not English may have problems in understanding. A simple step towards helping them to understand is to provide them with a list of key words and a translation into their own language. In addition, you can place multi-lingual labels on apparatus stored around the laboratory. You will generally find that past pupils are keen to help you produce these sorts of things if you can't do it yourself.

Practical activity 10.5

How could you use the BritKid website at *www.britkid.org/* to help pupils understand multi-cultural issues?

More black pupils than white pupils are excluded from school. One possible reason for this is teachers' lack of understanding of 'black culture'. Find out about the different types of cultures within your school and the approach teachers use when working with pupils.

Identify opportunities in the Science National Curriculum to raise multi-cultural issues and consider possible teaching approaches?

How could you use the Internet to give pupils a broader picture of science?

CONCLUSION

There will be many times in your career as a teacher that you will be amazed by the stories pupils tell you about their backgrounds. They all have interests or special talents that can be made use of in your science teaching. It is your job to find out what pupils can do and then make the most of it.

REFERENCES

ACCAC (2000) *Making Effective Use of Assessment Information: Reporting Key Stages 1–3*. Cardiff: ACCAC.

Adey, P.S. (1993) *Thinking Science INSET (The King's-BP CASE INSET Pack)*. London: BP Educational Services.

Adey, P.S. and Shayer, M. (1994) *Really Raising Standards: Cognitive Intervention and Academic Achievement*. London: Routledge.

Adey, P.S., Shayer, M. and Yates, C. (1989) *Thinking Science: The Curriculum Materials of the Cognitive Acceleration Through Science (CASE) Project*. London: Macmillan.

ASE (1996) *Safeguards in the School Laboratory* 10th edition. Hatfield: ASE.

 ASE (1999) *Science and the Literacy Hour*, an ASE report on the effect of the National Literacy Strategy on the teaching of science, *www.ase.org.uk/natlit1.html*

ASE (2001) *Topics in Safety*. Hatfield: ASE.

Assessment Reform Group (1999) *Assessment for Learning: Beyond the Black Box*. Cambridge: University of Cambridge School of Education.

Ausubel, D.P. (1968) *Educational Psychology: A Cognitive View*. New York: Holt, Rinehart and Winston.

Barker, V. (2000) *Beyond Appearances: Students' Misconceptions About Basic Chemical Ideas*. London: RSC. (This paper is available on the RSC Chem website at *www.chemsoc.org/networks/learnnet/miscon.htm*)

BECTa (2000) *Science On Line: Practical Ideas About Using the World Wide Web*. Coventry: BECTa *www.becta.org.uk/index.cfm*

Bishop, K. and Denley, P. (1997) *Effective Learning in Science*. Stafford: Network Educational Press.

Black, P. and Wiliam, D. (1998) Assessment and Classroom Learning, *Assessment in Education*, 5(1) 7–74.

Braund, M. (1999) Electric drama to improve understanding in science, *School Science Review*, 81(294), 35–41.

Bruner, J.S. (1986) *Actual Minds, Possible Worlds*. Cambridge, MA: Harvard University Press.

Canter, L. and Canter, M. (1993) *Succeeding With Difficult Students: New Strategies for Reaching Your Most Challenging Students*. Santa Monica: Lee Canter & Associates.

Capel, S., Leask, M. and Turner, T. (1995) *Learning to Teach in the Secondary School*. London: Routledge.

Car, D. (1998) The art of asking questions in the teaching of science, *School Science Review*, 79(289), 47–50.

Centre for Science Education, Sheffield City Polytechnic (1992) *Active Teaching and Learning Approaches in Science*. London: Collins.

Chapman, C., Musker, R., Nicholson, D. and Sheehan, M. (2000) *Eureka: Success in Science*. London: Heinemann.

Clark, C. and Callow, R. (1998) *Educating Able Children: Resource Issues and Processes for Teachers*. London: NACE/Fulton.

Clarke, S. (1998) *Targeting Assessment in the Primary Classroom*. London: Hodder & Stoughton.

CLEAPSS (2000a) *Student Safety Sheets*. Brunel University, London: CLEAPSS School Science Service.

CLEAPSS (2000b) *Hazcards*. Brunel University, London: CLEAPSS School Science Service.

Daws, N. and Singh, B. (1999) Formative Assessment Strategies in Secondary Science, *School Science Review*, 80(293), 71–8.

de Cicco, E., Farmer, M. and Hargrave, J. (1998) *Using the Internet in Secondary Schools*. London: Kogan Page.

DfEE (1996) *Safety in Science Education*. London: HMSO.

DfEE (1997) *Excellence in Schools*. London: HMSO.

DfEE and QCA (1999) *The National Curriculum: Handbook for Secondary Teachers in England*. London: HMSO.

Driver, R., Squires, A., Rushworth, P. and Wood-Robinson, V. (1994a) *Making Sense of Secondary Science: Support Materials for Teachers*. London: Routledge.

Driver, R., Squires, A., Rushworth, P. and Wood-Robinson, V. (1994b) *Making Sense of Secondary Science: Research into Children's Ideas*. London: Routledge.

Ellis, P. (1992) *Science Changes!* Wantage: PREtext Publishing.

Estyn (1999) *Primary and Secondary School Partnership: Improving Learning and Performance*. Cardiff: HMSO.

Estyn (2001) *Good Practice in Science*. Cardiff: HMSO.

Facer, K., Furlong, J., Sutherland, R. and Furlong, R. (2000) Home is where the hardware is: young people, the domestic environment and 'access' to new technologies. In Hutchby, I. and Moran-Ellis, J. (eds) *Children, Technology and Culture*. London: Falmer Press.

Flavell, J.H. (1963) *The Developmental Psychology of Jean Piaget*. New York: Van Nostrand.

Frost, R. (1999) *Data Logging in Practice*. London: IT in Science.

Frost, R. (2000) *The IT in Secondary Science Book*. London: IT in Science.

Frost, J. (with Jennings, A., Turner, T., Turner, S. and Beckett, L.) (1995) *Teaching Science*. London: Woburn Press.

Gaine, C. and George, R. (1999) *Gender, 'Race' and Class in Schooling: a New Introduction*. London: Falmer Press.

Galton, M., Gray, J. and Rudduck, J. (1999) *The Impact of School Transitions and Transfers on Pupil Progress and Attainment*. London: HMSO.

Gardner, H.C. (1983) *Frames of Mind: The Theory of Multiple Intelligence*. New York: Basic Books, *www.ed.psu.edu/insys/ESD/gardner/MItheory.html*

Goldsworthy, A., Watson, R. and Wood-Robinson, V. (1999) *Investigations: Getting to Grips with Graphs*. Hatfield: ASE.

Gott, R. and Duggan, S. (1995) *Investigative Work in the Science Curriculum*. Buckingham: Open University Press.

Hall, S. (1997) The problem with differentiation, *School Science Review*, 78(284), 95–8.

Harris, A., Jamieson, I. and Russ, J. (1996) *School Effectiveness and School Improvement*. London: Pitman.

Henderson, J. (2000) QCA key stage 3 science scheme of work – a teachers' view, *School Science Review*, 81(297), 23–7.

Ireson, J., Hallam, S., Mortimore, P., Hack, S., Clark, H. and Plewis, I.

(1999) Ability grouping in the secondary school: the effects on academic achievement and pupils' self-esteem. Paper presented at the BERA Conference, University of Sussex. Available at *www.leeds.ac.uk/educol/documents/00001359.htm*

Jerram, A. (1999) *Non-Specialist Handbook: Teaching Physics to KS4*. London: Hodder & Stoughton.

Jones, A.T., Simon, S.A., Black, P.J., Fairbrother, R.W. and Watson, J.R. (1992) *Open Work in Science: Development of Investigations in Schools*. Hatfield: ASE.

Kennewell, S., Parkinson, J. and Tanner, H. (2000) *Developing the ICT Captable School*. London: Routledge.

Kerry, T. (1998) *Questioning and Explaining in Classrooms*. London: Hodder & Stoughton.

Kerry, T. and Kerry, C.A. (1997) Differentiation: teachers' views of the usefulness of recommended strategies in helping the more able pupils in primary and secondary classrooms, *Educational Studies*, **23**(3), 439–57.

Kinchin, I.M. (2000a) Using concept maps to reveal understanding: a two-tier analysis, *School Science Review*, **81**(296), 41–6.

Kinchin, I.M. (2000b) Concept-mapping activities to help students understand photosyntheis – and teachers understand students, *School Science Review*, **82**(299), 11–14.

Koufetta-Menicou, C. and Scaife, J. (2000) Teachers' questions – types and significance in science education, *School Science Review*, **81**(296), 79–84.

Lawley, P. (1999) *Target Setting and Bench Marking*. London: Folens.

Learners' Cooperative, The (1998) *Differentiation Manual* 2nd edition. Plymouth: The Learners' Cooperative Ltd.

Leask, M. and Pachler, N. (1999) *Learning to Teach Using ICT in the Secondary School*. London: Routledge.

Maslow, A.H. (1987) *Motivation and Personality*. New York: Harper & Row.

McDuell, B. (ed.) (2000) *Teaching Secondary Chemistry*. London: ASE-John Murray.

McKeon, F. (2000) Literacy and secondary science – building on primary experience, *School Science Review*, **81**(297), 45–50.

McSharry, G. and Jones, S. (2000) Role-play in science teaching and learning, *School Science Review*, **82**(298), 73–82.

Monk, M. (2000) A critique of the QCA specimen scheme of work for key stage 3 science, *School Science Review*, **81**(297), 29–31.

Naylor, S. and Keogh, B. (2000) *Concept Cartoons in Science Education*. Sandbach: Millgate House.

Needham, R. (1987) *Teaching Strategies for Developing Understanding in Science*. Leeds: CLIS.

NIAS (Northampton Inspection and Advisory Service) (1995) *The Differentiation Book*. Northampton: The Science Centre.

Nott, M. and Wellington. J. (1999) The state we're in: issues in key stage 3 and 4 science, *School Science Review*, **81**(294), 13–18.

O'Brien, P. (2000) A challenging curriculum for the more able pupil. In Sears, J. and Sorensen, P. (eds) *Issues in Science Teaching*. London: Routledge Falmer.

Ofsted (2000a) *Inspecting Science 11–16 with Guidance on SELF-evaluation*. London: HMSO.

Ofsted (2000b) *Progress in Key Stage 3 Science*. London: HMSO.

Ofsted (2001) *Improving Attendance and Behaviour in Secondary Schools*. London: HMSO.

Osborne, J. and Collins, S. (2001) Students' views of the role and value of the science curriculum: a focus-group study, *International Journal of Science Education*, **23**(5), 441–67.

Osborne, J. and Simon, S. (1996) Primary science: past and future directions, *Studies in Science Education*, **27**, 99–147.

Parkinson, J. (1994) *The Effective Teaching of Secondary Science*. London: Longman.

Parkinson, J. and Rowe, M. (1997) Science. In Wilkin, M., Furlong, J., Miles, S. and Maynard, T. (eds) *The Subject Mentor Handbook for the Secondary School*. London: Kogan Page.

Perutz, M. (1998) *I Wish I'd Made You Angry Earlier: Essays on Science and Scientists*. Oxford: Oxford University Press.

Pollard, A. and Triggs, P. (1997) *Reflective Teaching in Secondary Education*. London: Continuum.

Pruden, V. (1999) *Assessing Sc1 for GCSE*. London: Heinemann.

 QCA Specimen SoWs for KS2 and KS3 science, available at *www.standards.dfes.gov.uk/schemes*

Ratcliffe, M. (1998) Discussing socio-scientific issues in science lessons – pupils' actions and the teachers' role, *School Science Review*, **79**(288), 55–9.

Reiss, M. (ed.) (1999) *Teaching Secondary Chemistry*. London: ASE-John Murray.

Ross, K., Lakin, L. and Callaghan, P. (2000) *Teaching Secondary Science: Constructing Meaning and Developing Understanding*. London: David Fulton.

Sang, D. (ed.) (2000a) *Teaching Secondary Chemistry*. London: ASE-John Murray.

 Sang, D. (ed.) (2000b) *Science@www:Getting Started*. Hatfield: ASE *www.ase.org.uk*

SATIS 16–19 (1990) Hatfield: ASE.

Schön, D.A. (1991) *The Reflective Practitioner: How Professionals Think in Action*. Aldershot: Arena.

School Science Review (1997) **79**(287).

Science Web Reader (2000) *Chemistry*. London: Nelson.

Scrimshaw, P. (ed.) (1993) *Language, Classrooms & Computers*. London: Routledge.

Selley, N. (2000) Wrong answers welcome, *School Science Review*, **92**(299), 41–4.

Shayer, M. and Adey, P.S. (1981) *Towards a Science of Science Teaching*. London: Heinemann.

Solomon, J. (1990) *Exploring the Nature of Science*. Glasgow: Blackie.

Stephenson, P. (1999) *Improving Experience in Science During Cross-Phase Transfer: A Perspective for ITT Providers*. Leicester: SCIcentre.

Sukhnandan, L. and Lee, B. (1998) *Streaming, Setting and Grouping by Ability*. Slough: NFER. Available at *www.nfer.ac.uk/summary/streaming.htm*

Swain, J.R.L. (1996) The impact and effect of key stage 3 science tests, *School Science Review*, **78**(283), 79–90.

Talbot, C. (2000) Ideas and evidence in science, *School Science Review*, 82(298), 13–22.

Tebbutt, M. and Flavell, H. (1995) *Spreadsheets in Science*. London: John Murray.

Torrance, H. and Prior, J. (1998) *Investigating Formative Assessment: Teaching Learning and Assessment in the Classroom*. Buckingham: Open University Press.

TTA (1999) *Improving Standards: Research and Evidence-Based Practice*. TTA publication 62/8–99. London: Teacher Training Agency (*www.canteach.gov. uk/publications/community/research/evidence/tta00_03.pdf*).

Vygotsky, L. (1978) Mind in Society: *The Development of Higher Psychological Processes*. Cambridge, MA: Harvard University Press.

Warren, D. (2001a) *The Nature of Science*. London: RSC.

Warren, D. (2001b) *Chemists in a Social and Historical Context*. London: RSC.

Watson, R., Goldsworthy, A. and Wood-Robinson, V. (1999) What is not fair with investigations?, *School Science Review*, 80(292), 101–6.

Wellington, J. (2000) *Teaching and Learning Secondary Science: Contemporary Issues and Practical Approaches*. London: Routledge.

Wilson, E. (1999) *Non-Specialist Handbook: Teaching Chemistry to KS4*. London: Hodder & Stoughton.

Winterbottom, M. (1999) *Non-Specialist Handbook: Teaching Biology to KS4*. London: Hodder & Stoughton.

World of Science, The (1997) New SATIS 14–16. London: John Murray.

INDEX